HOW TO FOLLOW GOD'S WILL

PART 2 OF 3

How to Follow God's Will
ISBN: 978-1-59548-161-0

Copyright © 2013 by Andrew Wommack Ministries, Inc.
P.O. Box 3333
Colorado Springs CO 80934-3333

www.awmi.net

TABLE OF CONTENTS

HOW TO USE YOUR STUDY GUIDE

HOW TO USE YOUR STUDY GUIDE

Whether you are teaching a class, leading a small group, discipling an individual, or studying on your own, this study guide is designed for you! Here's how it works:

Each study consists of a **Lesson, Outline, Teacher's Guide, Discipleship Questions, Answer Key**, and **Scriptures**—all of which have been divided into sections. Within the study, each section is a continuation of the previous section.

Outline for Group Study:
I. If possible, briefly review the previous study by going over the **Answer Key/Teacher's Guide** answers for the **Discipleship Questions/Teacher's Guide** questions.
II. Read the current section for the **Lesson** or **Teacher's Guide** aloud (e.g., 1.1, 1.2).
  A. Be sure that each student has a copy of the **Outline**.
  B. While the **Lesson** section or **Teacher's Guide** section is being read, students should use their **Outlines** to follow along.
III. Once the **Lesson** section or **Teacher's Guide** section is read, facilitate discussion and study using the **Discipleship Questions/Teacher's Guide** questions (the questions are all the same).
  A. Read aloud one question at a time.
  B. The group should use their **Outlines** to assist them in answering the questions.
  C. Have them read aloud each specifically mentioned scripture before answering the question.
  D. Discuss the answer/point from the **Lesson**, as desired.
  E. As much as possible, keep the discussion centered on the scriptures and the **Lesson** section or **Teacher's Guide** section points at hand.
  F. Remember, the goal is understanding (Matt. 13:19).
  G. One individual should not dominate the discussion, but try to draw out the quieter ones for the group conversation.
  H. Repeat the process until all of the questions are discussed/answered.

Materials Needed:
Study guide, Bible, and enough copies of the **Outline, Discipleship Questions**, and **Scriptures** for each student. (Printable files of the **Outline, Discipleship Questions**, and **Scriptures** can be found on the CD-ROM included with this book.)

Outline for Personal Study:
I. Read the current **Lesson** section or **Teacher's Guide** section.
  A. Read additional information, if provided.
  B. Meditate on the given scriptures, as desired.
II. Answer the corresponding **Discipleship Questions/Teacher's Guide** questions.
III. Check your work with the **Answer Key/Teacher's Guide** answers.

Materials Needed:
Study guide, Bible, and a writing utensil.

DELIGHT YOURSELF IN THE LORD

LESSON 6.1

God has a specific plan for every person. It's not hard to find His will for our lives, because He told us not to be ignorant but understand what the will of God is (Eph. 5:17). The Lord wants us to know His will for our lives, and it's absolutely essential for us to find it. We won't find God's will accidentally; we have to seek to find it (Matt. 7:7). Knowing God's will for our lives will allow us to set goals and help us persevere through difficulties. Finding God's will is essential, but it's only the starting point. There's a big difference between *finding* God's will and *following* it. After we discover what God's will for our life is, we have to purposely seek after it. We can't depend on fate to somehow make it happen.

I am going to discuss several things that will help you follow God's leading after you have found His will for your life. What I'm going to share is really simple, but it's dependent upon you continuing to make yourself a living sacrifice and renew your mind with the Word of God (as discussed in Part 1, *How to Find God's Will*). You never move beyond those first requirements. You can't make yourself a living sacrifice and renew your mind one time and never think about it again. Following and fulfilling God's will build upon the things that have already been discussed. If you are doing those things, then this simple but profound passage of Scripture will help you:

> *Trust in the LORD, and do good; so shalt thou dwell in the land, and verily thou shalt be fed. [4] Delight thyself also in the LORD; and he shall give thee the desires of thine heart. [5] Commit thy way unto the LORD; trust also in him; and he shall bring it to pass.*
>
> PSALM 37:3-5

When we delight ourselves in the Lord, He puts His desires in our hearts. Some people misinterpret this scripture to mean that God will give them whatever they want: a million-dollar house, a luxury car, a particular job, a promotion, or whatever. But this is not a free pass to get our hands on anything our flesh craves. Some people desire another person's spouse—God is not going to help them fulfill desires like that. As we seek the Lord with our whole hearts, He will change our hearts to desire godly things. Suddenly, the ungodly things we were doing before we gave our lives to the Lord won't appeal to us any longer. A lot of people experience this after they are born again.

The Hebrew word that was translated *"delight"* in Psalm 37:4 literally means "to be soft or pliable" (*Strong's Concordance*). It's speaking about having a sensitive heart toward the Lord. So, to delight in the Lord means to commit our lives to Him, to the degree that we are seeking His will and ways. It's putting Him first. If we do these things, God will order the desires of our hearts. But that's a big "if." I emphasize "if" because even though being totally committed to God is our normal Christian duty (Rom. 12:1), it's uncommon to see this. We Christians are by no means perfect, but we should desire to seek God with our whole hearts.

We all have to deal with our carnal nature and cope with the fact that we live in a sinful world and have thoughts and emotions that can lead us astray. I'm not saying that we have to live perfectly in order to be totally committed to God, but we should have a desire to live more for God than for ourselves. When we try to live for God, which is what it means to delight ourselves in the Lord, then God will put His desires in our hearts. It's pretty simple.

One of the most common ways that God leads us is by the desires of our hearts. Before we can trust our desires, we need to make sure that we're really delighting in the Lord. It isn't hard to tell if we are putting God first; all we have to do is be honest with ourselves. Proverbs says that the heart knows its own bitterness (Prov. 14:10). If God isn't first in our lives, we can't depend on being led by the desires of our hearts—we will lust after things that aren't godly. The desires of our hearts will not be the same as God's will for us unless we're delighting in Him.

Be Spiritually Minded

I was brought up in a legalistic church. When they taught on finding God's will, they actually said, "Whatever you want to do, do the exact opposite and that will be God." I don't recommend following that advice. But this is true for carnal Christians—people who make satisfying their own needs the greatest priority in their lives. The Bible says, *"The carnal mind is enmity against God: for it is not subject to the law of God, neither indeed can be"* (Rom. 8:7). So, it's true that people who don't pursue a relationship with God after they are born again can't trust their desires. Those who are just waiting on heaven might be saved, but they are stuck living by their carnal nature. Those believers can't trust the desires of their hearts to be godly.

Everyone who is truly committed to God can be led by the desires of their hearts. I could tell you a hundred stories from my life that show how God has led me in the best decisions I have ever made, just by using the simple principle of being led by my desires. For instance, I never wanted a Bible school. A lot of people asked me to start one, but I never wanted to—largely because I had met too many Bible school graduates who really annoyed me. They thought they were better than other Christians because they could quote Scripture. But they didn't have a better relationship with God or love God more than the people they looked down on. I didn't want to be associated with something like that, so I had no desire to start a Bible school—even though I have always had a strong desire to disciple people.

In the summer of 1993, I was in the U.K. and heard a man say that if you weren't training up people to do what God has shown you, you're a failure. It doesn't matter if you reach a hundred thousand people for Christ. Our time on earth is limited, so unless you can take what is in you and reproduce it in other people, then ultimately, you have failed. Christians are supposed to make disciples, not converts.

I knew those things were true, so it stirred something in me when I heard someone else preach about it. I thought, *God, how can I equip believers to help them start walking in the abundant life that You have made available?* The Lord answered me, "A Bible school." God showed me a new way to approach Bible school, and in one church service, the desires of my heart changed completely. I went from being totally opposed to having a Bible school to being really excited about the idea.

Charis Bible College grew from the desire God planted in my heart that day. The core of this program is two years of instruction, focusing on building a relationship with God while increasing one's scriptural knowledge. Today, we have several campuses in the United States and multiple extension schools around the world. Charis Bible College graduates are teaching and preaching in the United States, as well as doing great missionary work in Russia, Africa, India, South America, and other countries all over the globe.

I'm really excited about the future of the school and the impact graduates will make for the kingdom of God. And all of this began when God simply changed the desires of my heart. He didn't speak to me in an audible voice; I didn't have it confirmed by three goose bumps and a prophecy. God just led me by changing my desires.

I started on television in the same way. It was different in that I always knew I would be on television one day. I was very aware that television was a huge step. The expense associated with television is much more than the radio I had been doing for decades. I knew if God wasn't in this, I could destroy the foothold I had worked decades to secure. Although I knew it was in my future, I wasn't excited about taking that step.

In the summer of 1998, as I was thinking about where our ministry was, I realized that at the rate we were growing, it would take 150 years for us to reach all of America with the truths God had shown me—forget about trying to reach the rest of the world! I said, "God, You know this isn't working. What do we have to do?" All of a sudden I thought, *Television.* And the most amazing part was that I had a desire to do it.

Right then, I drew a picture of the set that we ended up using for the first twelve years of our television ministry. I saw what the program was going to look like. I knew I wasn't going to be wearing a three-piece suit, marching back and forth in front of a large crowd, and wiping the sweat from my brow as I preached. I saw how God wanted me to do it, so I became excited about television. It was 180-degree turn from where I was before God changed my desires.

Whenever my desires change suddenly like that and I think it might be God leading me in a new direction—especially if the potential consequences are big—I make sure that I am delighting myself in the Lord with all of my heart. When I'm not sure, I fast, turn off the television, get away from other people, and try to focus my mind on God as best as I can. I worship, pray, study the Word, and seek God stronger than I have been. In other words, I seek God with my whole heart.

As I seek God, the desire in my heart either increases or decreases. If the desire gets smaller, I conclude that it was probably a carnal desire of my flesh. But if the desire keeps getting stronger and I start getting further revelation as I seek God with all of my heart, I know God is leading me. I have based my life on the knowledge that when I am seeking God and delighting myself in the Lord, He puts His desires in my heart. Some of the biggest decisions of my life were based on nothing more than seeking God first and following the desires in my heart.

I promise you that this principle works. God is doing awesome things for us. I am absolutely confident that I am on the right path. I haven't arrived, but praise God, I've left. I'm moving in the right direction. I know I'm where God wants me to be. This is how you get there: Put God first in your life and then follow the desires of your heart. Unfortunately, most people do not follow their hearts. They let conventional wisdom dominate them. They allow circumstances and money to dictate their course in life instead of following the desires of their hearts.

OUTLINE • 6.1

I.   God has a specific plan for every person.

      A.   It's not hard to find His will for our lives, because He told us not to be ignorant but understand what the will of God is (Eph. 5:17).

      B.   Knowing God's will for our lives will allow us to set goals and help us persevere through difficulties.

      C.   There's a big difference between *finding* God's will and *following* it.

      D.   What I'm going to share in this study guide is really simple, but it's dependent upon us continuing to make ourselves living sacrifices and renew our minds with the Word of God.

II.   When we delight ourselves in the Lord, He puts His desires in our hearts.

> *Trust in the LORD, and do good; so shalt thou dwell in the land, and verily thou shalt be fed. [4] Delight thyself also in the LORD; and he shall give thee the desires of thine heart. [5] Commit thy way unto the LORD; trust also in him; and he shall bring it to pass.*
>
> PSALM 37:3-5

      A.   But this is not a free pass to get our hands on anything our flesh craves.

      B.   The Hebrew word that was translated *"delight"* in Psalm 37:4 literally means "to be soft or pliable" (*Strong's Concordance*).

      C.   So, to delight in the Lord means to commit our lives to Him, to the degree that we are seeking His will and ways.

      D.   I'm not saying that we have to live perfectly in order to be totally committed to God, but we should have a desire to live more for God than for ourselves.

      E.   When we try to live for God, which is what it means to delight ourselves in the Lord, then God will put His desires in our hearts—it's pretty simple.

      F.   Before we can trust our desires, we need to make sure that we're really delighting in the Lord.

      G.   If God isn't first in our lives, we can't depend on being led by the desires of our hearts—we will lust after things that aren't godly.

III.   I was brought up in a legalistic church, and when they taught on finding God's will, they actually said, "Whatever you want to do, do the exact opposite and that will be God."

      A.   I don't recommend following that advice, but this is true for carnal Christians—people who make satisfying their own needs the greatest priority in their lives.

B. The Bible says, *"The carnal mind is enmity against God: for it is not subject to the law of God, neither indeed can be"* (Rom. 8:7).

C. So, it's true that people who don't pursue a relationship with God after they are born again can't trust their desires.

D. But everyone who is truly committed to God can be led by the desires of their hearts.

E. For instance, I never wanted a Bible school; but God showed me a new way to approach Bible school, and in one church service, the desires of my heart changed completely.

F. God just led me by changing my desires.

G. Whenever my desires change suddenly like that and I think it might be God leading me in a new direction—especially if the potential consequences are big—I make sure that I am delighting myself in the Lord with all of my heart.

H. As I seek God, the desire in my heart either increases or decreases.

   i.   If the desire gets smaller, I conclude that it was probably a carnal desire of my flesh.

   ii. But if the desire keeps getting stronger and I start getting further revelation as I seek God with all of my heart, I know God is leading me.

I. I promise you that this principle works.

1. God has a specific plan for every person. It's not hard to find His will for our lives, because He told us not to be ignorant but understand what the will of God is (Eph. 5:17). Knowing God's will for our lives will allow us to set goals and help us persevere through difficulties. There's a big difference between *finding* God's will and *following* it. What I'm going to share in this study guide is really simple, but it's dependent upon us continuing to make ourselves living sacrifices and renew our minds with the Word of God.

1a. Discussion question: Read Ephesians 5:17. Why is it so important to understand what the will of the Lord is?
Discussion question

1b. There's a big difference between _____ God's will and _____ it.
A. Finding / following
B. Guessing / living
C. Discerning / ignoring
D. Loving / sharing
E. Embracing / heeding
A. Finding / following

1c. True or false: Following God's will has nothing to do with making yourself a living sacrifice and renewing your mind with the Word of God.
False

2. When we delight ourselves in the Lord, He puts His desires in our hearts.

> *Trust in the LORD, and do good; so shalt thou dwell in the land, and verily thou shalt be fed. [4] Delight thyself also in the LORD; and he shall give thee the desires of thine heart. [5] Commit thy way unto the LORD; trust also in him; and he shall bring it to pass.*
>
> PSALM 37:3-5

But this is not a free pass to get our hands on anything our flesh craves. The Hebrew word that was translated *"delight"* in Psalm 37:4 literally means "to be soft or pliable" (*Strong's Concordance*). So, to delight in the Lord means to commit our lives to Him, to the degree that we are seeking His will and ways. I'm not saying that we have to live perfectly in order to be totally committed to God, but we should have a desire to live more for God than for ourselves. When we try to live for God, which is what it means to delight ourselves in the Lord, then God will put His desires in our hearts—it's pretty simple. Before we can trust our desires, we need to make sure that we're really delighting in the Lord. If God isn't first in our lives, we can't depend on being led by the desires of our hearts—we will lust after things that aren't godly.

2a. Read Psalm 37:3-5. What happens when you delight yourself in the Lord?
He puts His desires in your heart

2b. Discussion question: What does the definition of *"delight"* ("to be soft or pliable" [*Strong's Concordance*]) mean to you?
Discussion question

2c. True or false: You don't have to live perfectly in order to be totally committed to God.
True

3. I was brought up in a legalistic church, and when they taught on finding God's will, they actually said, "Whatever you want to do, do the exact opposite and that will be God." I don't recommend following that advice, but this is true for carnal Christians—people who make satisfying their own needs the greatest priority in their lives. The Bible says, *"The carnal mind is enmity against God: for it is not subject to the law of God, neither indeed can be"* (Rom. 8:7). So, it's true that people who don't pursue a relationship with God after they are born again can't trust their desires. But everyone who is truly committed to God can be led by the desires of their hearts. For instance, I never wanted a Bible school; but God showed me a new way to approach Bible school, and in one church service, the desires of my heart changed completely. God just led me by changing my desires. Whenever my desires change suddenly like that and I think it might be God leading me in a new direction—especially if the potential consequences are big—I make sure that I am delighting myself in the Lord with all of my heart. As I seek God, the desire in my heart either increases or decreases. If the desire gets smaller, I conclude that it was probably a carnal desire of my flesh. But if the desire keeps getting stronger and I start getting further revelation as I seek God with all of my heart, I know God is leading me. I promise you that this principle works.

3a. What is the definition of a carnal Christian?
     A person who makes satisfying their own needs the greatest priority in their lives

3b. Discussion question: Read Romans 8:7. What do you think are some attributes of a *"carnal mind"*?
     Discussion question

3c. But everyone who is truly _____ to God can be _____ by the desires of their hearts.
     Committed / led

3d. How can you know that the desire in your heart is of God?
     A. By fasting and repeating the Lord's Prayer
     B. By delighting yourself in the Lord with all of your heart
     C. By hoping and guessing
     D. All of the above
     E. None of the above
     B. By delighting yourself in the Lord with all of your heart

DISCIPLESHIP QUESTIONS • 6.1

1. Discussion question: Read Ephesians 5:17. Why is it so important to understand what the will of the Lord is?

_____

_____

_____

2. There's a big difference between _____ God's will and _____ it.
   A. Finding / following
   B. Guessing / living
   C. Discerning / ignoring
   D. Loving / sharing
   E. Embracing / heeding

3. True or false: Following God's will has nothing to do with making yourself a living sacrifice and renewing your mind with the Word of God.

4. Read Psalm 37:3-5. What happens when you delight yourself in the Lord?

_____

_____

_____

5. Discussion question: What does the definition of *"delight"* ("to be soft or pliable" [*Strong's Concordance*]) mean to you?

_____

_____

_____

6. True or false: You don't have to live perfectly in order to be totally committed to God.

7. What is the definition of a carnal Christian?

_____

_____

_____

8. Discussion question: Read Romans 8:7. What do you think are some attributes of a *"carnal mind"*?

_____

_____

_____

9. But everyone who is truly _____ to God can be _____ by the desires of their hearts.

10. How can you know that the desire in your heart is of God?
    A. By fasting and repeating the Lord's Prayer
    B. By delighting yourself in the Lord with all of your heart
    C. By hoping and guessing
    D. All of the above
    E. None of the above

ANSWER KEY • 6.1

1. *Discussion question*
2. A. Finding / following
3. False
4. He puts His desires in your heart
5. *Discussion question*
6. True
7. A person who makes satisfying their own needs the greatest priority in their lives
8. *Discussion question*
9. Committed / led
10. B. By delighting yourself in the Lord with all of your heart

EPHESIANS 5:17
Wherefore be ye not unwise, but understanding what the will of the Lord is.

MATTHEW 7:7
Ask, and it shall be given you; seek, and ye shall find; knock, and it shall be opened unto you.

PSALM 37:3-5
Trust in the LORD, and do good; so shalt thou dwell in the land, and verily thou shalt be fed. [4] Delight thyself also in the LORD; and he shall give thee the desires of thine heart. [5] Commit thy way unto the LORD; trust also in him; and he shall bring it to pass.

ROMANS 12:1
I beseech you therefore, brethren, by the mercies of God, that ye present your bodies a living sacrifice, holy, acceptable unto God, which is your reasonable service.

PROVERBS 14:10
The heart knoweth his own bitterness; and a stranger doth not intermeddle with his joy.

ROMANS 8:7
Because the carnal mind is enmity against God: for it is not subject to the law of God, neither indeed can be.

LESSON 6.2

Forget your fears and phobias about what you can or cannot do. For a moment, forget all of your financial obligations and how far away from retirement you are. Remove every restriction that is holding you back. Now, what do you want to do? Are you doing what you really want to be doing with your life?

The majority of people whom I have asked this question to say they are not doing what they really want to do. Life is too short for that. I tell people if they aren't living on the edge, they are taking up too much space. You need to be out there. You need to be doing something. Life isn't a dress rehearsal. You don't get a second shot at life. Is anybody going to miss you when you're gone? Have you made a difference? If you are truly putting God first, then your desires are telling you what you were born to do. Your heart knows what your purpose in life is.

We preach a lot on vision at Charis Bible College; therefore, I've had students come to me when it gets close to the end of school and say, "I still don't know what God wants me to do. I've prayed, but I haven't heard a thing." So, I sit down with them and tell them what I have just told you: Forget about money for right now, act like you have billions of dollars and money is not even an issue, forget about what your relatives and friends are saying, forget about past experiences that have made you feel like a failure—forget about all of that stuff. If there were no restrictions on you, what would you want to do?

Sometimes people aren't sure. But everybody, I mean everybody, has desires on the inside of them. Every person I have ever counseled with had a dream of some kind. Once they got over all of their phobias and out of the mindset of trying to do what everyone else expected them to do, they started to express their dreams. I have talked to dozens, maybe hundreds of people, who really did have a word from God, but they didn't trust their own desires. They thought the desire was coming from them, so they dismissed it. Most of us would rather have an angel appear to us, or a burning bush speak to us, and tell us what to do.

I have never heard the audible voice of God. I'm not saying God doesn't speak to people in a voice that is heard like conversation, but it's not how He typically communicates. Usually, it's as simple as putting God first in your life, seeking Him with your whole heart, and following the desires of your heart. Again, you have to check those desires against the Word of God. The desire to rob a bank or commit some other sin obviously doesn't come from God. However, if the desire of your heart increases the more you seek God and pray, you need to follow it.

I think a lot of people have let life beat the dreams out of them. They have been disappointed so many times, so they don't want to put themselves out on a limb and risk being disappointed again. Other people feel like dreaming is for kids, so they put their dreams on a shelf in order to pursue what the world values. But God didn't create us to trudge through life just trying to make ends meet. Life is meant to be exciting. We are meant to know the joy of feeling like our lives are making a difference.

Serving God is not boring. If you're bored, you haven't found God's will for your life. Following God's will is like riding a roller coaster: There's excitement at every curve. You will face challenges and be stretched. Not everyone is supposed to be in full-time ministry, trying to reach millions of people, but everyone should be excited about the future and what they are doing. God didn't create anyone to just occupy space.

The Body of Christ

When I was in Lamar, Colorado, I had a Bible study. There were seven sisters who attended this particular Bible study. They were all fanatical about God. One time, the young son of one of these sisters pulled a motorcycle on top of himself, and it crushed his chest. The sister just pushed his chest back into its normal shape and prayed over him for about thirty minutes. She commanded him to live, and he came back to life.

Another time, the mother of these seven sisters died, so they prayed over her and she was raised from the dead. Then their mother stood up, walked two miles into town, bought groceries, and came back. These sisters aren't on television—they aren't even preachers—but they are walking in the supernatural power of God. Their town knows who they are and people have been born again because of their testimony. They are making a difference. Their lives count!

God doesn't want everybody to be full-time preachers or teachers, but He wants us all to be ministers of His love. He wants all of us to live lives that make an impact for the kingdom of God. Our lives should count. We should be part of a church where we can be involved in something bigger than ourselves. The American dream of building our own personal empire is not God's dream. God wants our lives to impact others in a positive way.

Nobody lies on their deathbed and says, "Oh, I wish I had owned a bigger house and nicer cars. I wish I had more diamonds and jewels." The regrets people have at the end of their lives involve relationship failures. People regret that their lives didn't make a bigger impact, because life is all about relationships. God is in the people business. Whatever God's purpose for your life is, somehow or another, it is going to relate to changing people.

One of my employees had a friend who believed beyond any shadow of a doubt that God led him into the garbage collecting business. He rightly pointed out that somebody has to collect the garbage—it would be unhealthy if you didn't. This guy would straighten up everyone's garbage can and always leave things nice and tidy. He took pride in what he did and used collecting garbage as an opportunity to witness the love of God. He felt fulfilled because every day, he had the opportunity to show somebody the kindness of God or tell somebody about the Lord. Every believer has that same supernatural love and power of God. No matter what God has called you to do, you can use His love and power to impact the lives around you.

Get Out of the Boat

God will lead you in multiple ways, but probably the number one way you learn how to follow God's will is simply by putting Him first and following the desires He puts in your heart. When you delight yourself in the Lord, He changes the desires of your heart to align with your purpose. You can trust those desires. This is how God will lead you most of the time. He is not likely to speak to you in an audible voice or appear to you in a visible form. That's why it takes faith to follow God's leading.

> *But without faith it is impossible to please him: for he that cometh to God must believe that he is, and that he is a rewarder of them that diligently seek him.*
> HEBREWS 11:6

God delights in revealing Himself in subtle ways. Jesus could have come to earth on a 747 jet and landed in Jerusalem, but He chose to come meekly instead. Joseph had to take it by faith that Mary had gotten pregnant by the Holy Spirit and not through a natural human relationship. When Jesus rose from the dead, He could have hovered over Jerusalem to prove to everyone who crucified Him that He was alive again. Instead, after Jesus rose from the dead, He only appeared to people who already believed in Him. Jesus could have forced people to recognize His resurrection, but that's not how God does things. He wants people to believe by faith. He doesn't force His will on anybody.

If you are putting God first, then He has been trying to lead you by putting His desires in your heart. But you have to get out of the boat. You have to take a step and get out on the water. Be bold enough to step out and follow the desires of your heart. Your life will take on meaning; it will be exciting! You will make an impact in the lives of others. It will be worth the risk of getting out of your comfort zone.

You might be thinking, *I'm afraid I'll sink. I should just stay in the boat.* When Peter stepped out of the boat to walk toward Jesus on the sea (Matt. 14:24-33), the boat was already full of water. They were all about to drown. There was very little difference between being in the boat and being out of the boat. Many believers are afraid of stepping out and following God's leading, yet they are miserable. They are stuck in the same rut as everyone else—work, television, and sleep—but they won't do anything to change. What do you have to lose? At least when you are out of the boat, you will be following God. You'll be taking a chance. In order to walk on water, you have to get out of the boat!

You need to use wisdom in order to do what God leads you to do in His timing. Don't just sit still and wait for it to happen on its own. Do something. Take a step. When someone feels led to come to Charis Bible College but they can't see how it is going to work out, I tell them to put down the registration fee and see what happens. It's a step. Once you get the boat moving, even if it is barely moving, the rudder can change its course. But if the boat is motionless, you can flip the rudder 360 degrees and never change direction. You have to do something for God to steer you. If you aren't totally sure, don't go full-steam ahead—move slowly. Just start doing something.

The book of 2 Kings tells the story of four lepers who sat at the entrance to the besieged city of Samaria. Inside the city, there was famine; the citizens were eating cow dung and even their own children, in some cases. The enemy had the city surrounded, and their supplies were cut off. The lepers said,

> *Why sit we here until we die? [4] If we say, We will enter into the city, then the famine is in the city, and we shall die there: and if we sit still here, we die also. Now therefore come, and let us fall unto the host of the Syrians: if they save us alive, we shall live; and if they kill us, we shall but die.*
>
> 2 KINGS 7:3-4

The lepers knew that heading down toward the enemy camp was dangerous, but they realized they were going to die anyway. At least by taking a risk, they had a chance of surviving. So, they went out to the camp of the Syrians. When they arrived, they discovered the Lord had already defeated the enemy. The entire camp was deserted, and their food was still cooking on the fire. They found gold, silver, and raiment and became instantly wealthy. After their discovery, the lepers returned to the city to share the good news of how the enemy had fled.

Those four lepers brought deliverance to the entire city of Samaria. They became heroes because somebody finally said, "How long am I going to sit here—until I die?" It's better to take a step of faith and fail than to sit around doing nothing and call it success. God can bless you doing the wrong thing—because you are trying to move in faith—more than He can bless you doing nothing out of fear, which is unbelief. If God has put a desire in your heart, don't sit around waiting until you die. Do something about it!

I hope you can feel the Holy Spirit trying to stir you up. You need to be stirred up—if you aren't, you will settle to the bottom. God wants you to reach your full potential. When my life is over, I want to look back and say, "Father, thank You, I've run the race. I've finished the course (2 Tim. 4:7). I gave it everything I had." I don't want to reach the end of my life and say, "I wish I had done what was really in my heart." To the best of my ability, I'm doing what's in my heart. I want to encourage you to do the same. You won't ever arrive, but you need to leave the station.

It isn't enough just to find God's will. You have to begin to take steps to follow His leading. Being in the center of God's will brings a sense of satisfaction that you will never experience when you are out of His will. It doesn't matter if you love God and live a holy life. You still need to be where God wants you to be in order to experience the satisfaction and contentment that only come from being in His will.

The main way God has directed me into the center of His will has been by the desires of my heart. As you seek God first in your life, He will put His desires in your heart—then it's up to you to act on your desires. You don't have to make an all-out charge toward what God is leading you to do, if you aren't certain. Just take a few steps toward the desire in your heart. The Lord delights in faith, and when you begin to step out in faith, He will show Himself strong on your behalf (2 Chr. 16:9).

IV.   Remove every restriction that is holding you back—now, what do you want to do?

    A. The majority of people whom I have asked this question to say they are not doing what they really want to do; life is too short for that.

    B. You don't get a second shot at life.

    C. Your heart knows what your purpose in life is.

    D. Every person I have ever counseled with had a dream of some kind, but they thought the desire was coming from them, so they dismissed it.

    E. Most would rather have an angel appear to them, or a burning bush speak to them, and tell them what to do.

    F. I'm not saying God doesn't speak to people in a voice that is heard like conversation, but it's not how He typically communicates.

    G. Usually, it's as simple as putting God first in your life, seeking Him with your whole heart, and following the desires of your heart.

    H. God didn't create you to trudge through life just trying to make ends meet—life is meant to be exciting.

    I. Not everyone is supposed to be in full-time ministry, trying to reach millions of people, but everyone should be excited about the future and what they are doing.

    J. God didn't create anyone to just occupy space.

V.   God doesn't want everybody to be full-time preachers or teachers, but He wants us all to be ministers of His love.

    A. He wants all of us to live lives that make an impact for the kingdom of God—our lives should count.

    B. The American dream of building our own personal empire is not God's dream.

    C. Nobody lies on their deathbed and wishes for more possessions.

    D. People regret that their lives didn't make a bigger impact, because life is all about relationships.

    E. Whatever God's purpose for our lives is, somehow or another, it is going to relate to changing people.

    F. No matter what God has called us to do, we can use His love and power to impact the lives around us.

VI. God is not likely to speak to you in an audible voice or appear to you in a visible form.

    A. That's why it takes faith to follow God's leading.

       But without faith it is impossible to please him: for he that cometh to God must believe that he is, and that he is a rewarder of them that diligently seek him.
       HEBREWS 11:6

    B. God delights in revealing Himself in subtle ways—He wants people to believe by faith.

    C. He doesn't force His will on anybody.

    D. If you are putting God first, then He has been trying to lead you by putting His desires in your heart, but you have to get out of the boat (Matt. 14:24-33).

    E. Many believers are afraid of stepping out and following God's leading, yet they are miserable.

    F. At least when you are out of the boat, you will be following God.

    G. If you aren't totally sure, don't go full-steam ahead—move slowly.

    H. Just start doing something.

    I. It's better to take a step of faith and fail than to sit around doing nothing and call it success.

    J. God can bless you doing the wrong thing—because you are trying to move in faith—more than He can bless you doing nothing out of fear, which is unbelief.

    K. You don't have to make an all-out charge toward what God is leading you to do, if you aren't certain.

    L. The Lord delights in faith, and when you begin to step out in faith, He will show Himself strong on your behalf (2 Chr. 16:9).

4. Remove every restriction that is holding you back—now, what do you want to do? The majority of people whom I have asked this question to say they are not doing what they really want to do; life is too short for that. You don't get a second shot at life. Your heart knows what your purpose in life is. Every person I have ever counseled with had a dream of some kind, but they thought the desire was coming from them, so they dismissed it. Most would rather have an angel appear to them, or a burning bush speak to them, and tell them what to do. I'm not saying God doesn't speak to people in a voice that is heard like conversation, but it's not how He typically communicates. Usually, it's as simple as putting God first in your life, seeking Him with your whole heart, and following the desires of your heart. God didn't create you to trudge through life just trying to make ends meet—life is meant to be exciting. Not everyone is supposed to be in full-time ministry, trying to reach millions of people, but everyone should be excited about the future and what they are doing. God didn't create anyone to just occupy space.

4a.   Discussion question: What do you really want to do?
Discussion question

4b.   True or false: You get more than one shot at life.
False

4c.   What *didn't* God create you to do?
Trudge through life, just trying to make ends meet, and just occupy space

5.   God doesn't want everybody to be full-time preachers or teachers, but He wants us all to be ministers of His love. He wants all of us to live lives that make an impact for the kingdom of God—our lives should count. The American dream of building our own personal empire is not God's dream. Nobody lies on their deathbed and wishes for more possessions. People regret that their lives didn't make a bigger impact, because life is all about relationships. Whatever God's purpose for our lives is, somehow or another, it is going to relate to changing people. No matter what God has called us to do, we can use His love and power to impact the lives around us.

5a.   True or false: God wants everybody to be full-time preachers or teachers.
False

5b.   Discussion question: What does it mean to live a life that makes an impact for the kingdom of God and make your life count?
Discussion question

5c.   No matter what God has called you to do, you can use _____ love and power to impact the lives around you.
His

6. God is not likely to speak to you in an audible voice or appear to you in a visible form. That's why it takes faith to follow God's leading.

> *But without faith it is impossible to please him: for he that cometh to God must believe that he is, and that he is a rewarder of them that diligently seek him.*
> HEBREWS 11:6

God delights in revealing Himself in subtle ways—He wants people to believe by faith. He doesn't force His will on anybody. If you are putting God first, then He has been trying to lead you by putting His desires in your heart, but you have to get out of the boat (Matt. 14:24-33). Many believers are afraid of stepping out and following God's leading, yet they are miserable. At least when you are out of the boat, you will be following God. If you aren't totally sure, don't go full-steam ahead—move slowly. Just start doing something. It's better to take a step of faith and fail than to sit around doing nothing and call it success. God can bless you doing the wrong thing—because you are trying to move in faith—more than He can bless you doing nothing out of fear, which is unbelief. You don't have to make an all-out charge toward what God is leading you to do, if you aren't certain. The Lord delights in faith, and when you begin to step out in faith, He will show Himself strong on your behalf (2 Chr. 16:9).

6a. Why does it take faith to follow God's leading?
Because God is not likely to speak to you in an audible voice or appear to you in a visible form

6b. Discussion question: Read Hebrews 11:6. Why do you think it is impossible to please God without faith?
Discussion question

6c. Discussion question: Read Matthew 14:24-33. What can you learn from Peter's experience of walking on water?
Discussion question

6d. It's better to do what?
   A. Play it safe and stay where you are than to take a chance and try something new.
   B. Take a step of faith and fail than to sit around doing nothing and call it success.
   C. Convince others to do the work of the ministry for you than to do it yourself.
   D. All of the above
   E. None of the above
   B. Take a step of faith and fail than to sit around doing nothing and call it success

11. Discussion question: What do you really want to do?

_____

_____

_____

12. True or false: You get more than one shot at life.

13. What *didn't* God create you to do?

_____

_____

_____

14. True or false: God wants everybody to be full-time preachers or teachers.

15. Discussion question: What does it mean to live a life that makes an impact for the kingdom of God and make your life count?

_____

_____

_____

16. No matter what God has called you to do, you can use _____ love and power to impact the lives around you.

17. Why does it take faith to follow God's leading?

_____

_____

_____

18. Discussion question: Read Hebrews 11:6. Why do you think it is impossible to please God without faith?

_____

_____

_____

19. Discussion question: Read Matthew 14:24-33. What can you learn from Peter's experience of walking on water?

_____

_____

_____

20. It's better to do what?
    A. Play it safe and stay where you are than to take a chance and try something new.
    B. Take a step of faith and fail than to sit around doing nothing and call it success.
    C. Convince others to do the work of the ministry for you than to do it yourself.
    D. All of the above
    E. None of the above

ANSWER KEY • 6.2

11. *Discussion question*
12. False
13. Trudge through life, just trying to make ends meet, and just occupy space
14. False
15. *Discussion question*
16. His
17. Because God is not likely to speak to you in an audible voice or appear to you in a visible form
18. *Discussion question*
19. *Discussion question*
20. B.   Take a step of faith and fail than to sit around doing nothing and call it success.

HEBREWS 11:6
But without faith it is impossible to please him: for he that cometh to God must believe that he is, and that he is a rewarder of them that diligently seek him.

MATTHEW 14:24-33
But the ship was now in the midst of the sea, tossed with waves: for the wind was contrary. [25] And in the fourth watch of the night Jesus went unto them, walking on the sea. [26] And when the disciples saw him walking on the sea, they were troubled, saying, It is a spirit; and they cried out for fear. [27] But straightway Jesus spake unto them, saying, Be of good cheer; it is I; be not afraid. [28] And Peter answered him and said, Lord, if it be thou, bid me come unto thee on the water. [29] And he said, Come. And when Peter was come down out of the ship, he walked on the water, to go to Jesus. [30] But when he saw the wind boisterous, he was afraid; and beginning to sink, he cried, saying, Lord, save me. [31] And immediately Jesus stretched forth his hand, and caught him, and said unto him, O thou of little faith, wherefore didst thou doubt? [32] And when they were come into the ship, the wind ceased. [33] Then they that were in the ship came and worshipped him, saying, Of a truth thou art the Son of God.

2 KINGS 7:3-4
And there were four leprous men at the entering in of the gate: and they said one to another, Why sit we here until we die? [4] If we say, We will enter into the city, then the famine is in the city, and we shall die there: and if we sit still here, we die also. Now therefore come, and let us fall unto the host of the Syrians: if they save us alive, we shall live; and if they kill us, we shall but die.

2 TIMOTHY 4:7
I have fought a good fight, I have finished my course, I have kept the faith.

2 CHRONICLES 16:9
For the eyes of the LORD run to and fro throughout the whole earth, to shew himself strong in the behalf of them whose heart is perfect toward him. Herein thou hast done foolishly: therefore from henceforth thou shalt have wars.

TIMING AND PREPARATION

LESSON 7.1

Moses was a great man of God. He pursued God's will for his life with tremendous dedication, but he also made some major mistakes along the way. He caused himself, along with the entire Jewish nation, a lot of grief. Moses had a revelation of God's will for his life but he didn't have a clue how to fulfill it. As a result, he tried doing things his own way and caused a lot of problems. Moses is a prime example of why learning how to cooperate with God is a key element in following His leading.

When Moses was born, Pharaoh had given an order to kill all of the male children born to the Israelites (Ex. 1:15-16). During this time, the population of the Israelites was multiplying greatly and Pharaoh was afraid they would take over the land of Egypt, so he ordered the midwives to kill all the male children.

I find it interesting that every time in history when a dominant godly leader was about to come on the scene, such as Jesus or Moses, there was a move by the government to kill infants (Matt. 2:16). It's like Satan could tell that something was coming, and he tried to stop it by killing the babies. In our own time, there have been over fifty million babies aborted since 1973 in the United States alone. In fact, abortion is the leading cause of death in America—it kills almost twice as many people annually as heart disease, while accounting for 39 percent of all deaths in America 2005.

The sad part is that abortion is being promoted around the world as a solution to unwanted pregnancies. You just can't ignore the fact that there's a huge movement to kill infants. I believe it's because we are at the end time. Just as when Moses and Jesus were born, Satan is trying to prevent God from carrying out the final stages in His plan of redemption— but God always has a way to circumvent Satan's evil schemes.

God was able to preserve Moses through the time of infanticide in Egypt. His parents kept him for three months, and when they couldn't hide him any longer, his mother put him in a basket daubed with pitch and let it drift down along the edge of the Nile River. Moses' sister watched from a distance to see what would happen. Pharaoh's daughter went down to the river to bathe, saw the basket among the rushes, and discovered Moses. She knew he had to be one of the Hebrew children, so she took him and raised him as her own.

I love how God operates: Satan was trying to kill the Israelites' potential leader—using Pharaoh as his instrument—so God sent the leader directly to Pharaoh to supply his upbringing, education, and training. God always has a way of getting His will accomplished.

> And it came to pass in those days, when Moses was grown, that he went out unto his brethren, and looked on their burdens: and he spied an Egyptian smiting an Hebrew, one of his brethren. [12] And he looked this way and that way, and when he saw that there was no man, he slew the Egyptian, and hid him in the sand. [13] And when he went out the second day, behold, two men of the Hebrews strove together: and he said to him that did the wrong, Wherefore smitest thou thy fellow? [14] And he said, Who made thee a prince and a judge over us? intendest thou to kill me, as thou killedst the Egyptian? And Moses feared, and said, Surely this thing is known. [15] Now when Pharaoh heard this thing, he sought to slay Moses. But Moses fled from the face of Pharaoh, and dwelt in the land of Midian: and he sat down by a well.
>
> EXODUS 2:11-15

This small amount of information summarizes the first forty years of Moses' life. I like the old movie *The Ten Commandments*, but it is totally inaccurate in a lot of its details. The movie seems to rely solely on the book of Exodus for its account of Moses' life, but to truly understand the story of Moses, you need information that is only provided in the New Testament. Without that information, some inaccurate conclusions will be drawn. In the books of Acts and Hebrews, the Holy Spirit inspired the authors to write about Moses and fill in the details that you don't get by reading the book of Exodus. The Bible is its own commentary—that's a good principle to remember.

The Ten Commandments portrays that Moses sort of fell into his destiny when he saw an Egyptian beating a Hebrew. Then, out of a sense of right and wrong, he defended the Hebrew by killing the Egyptian. The movie conveys a common misconception that Moses didn't know that he was a Jew; however, Scripture shows otherwise—Moses *did* know his heritage.

Stephen was the first Christian martyr. Right before he was stoned to death, he recounted Jewish history to the council to show that he wasn't against the Jewish faith. He started with Abraham and went on through the promises and prophecies that were given to the Jews about the coming of the Messiah. Stephen was speaking under the inspiration of the Holy

Spirit, and the things he said fill in the blanks to give us a better understanding of what actually happened to Moses. He said,

> *In which time Moses was born, and was exceeding fair, and nourished up in his father's house three months:* **[21]** *And when he was cast out, Pharaoh's daughter took him up, and nourished him for her own son.* **[22]** *And Moses was learned in all the wisdom of the Egyptians, and was mighty in words and in deeds.* **[23]** *And when he was full forty years old, it came into his heart to visit his brethren the children of Israel.*
>
> ACTS 7:20-23

This is the only place in the Bible where we learn that Moses was forty years old when he killed the Egyptian. It says when he was forty years old, *"it came into his heart to visit his brethren, the children of Israel."* This reflects what I taught about delighting in the Lord and God putting His desires in our hearts. Moses knew he was a Jew. He saw the oppression of the Jews and related to it. God put it in his heart to go and visit his brethren. Moses didn't find himself among the Jews accidentally when he saw the Hebrew man being beaten; it was in his heart to be there.

Timing Is Everything

> *And seeing one of them suffer wrong, he defended him, and avenged him that was oppressed, and smote the Egyptian:* **[25]** *For he supposed his brethren would have understood how that God by his hand would deliver them: but they understood not.*
>
> ACTS 7:24-25

This verse makes it crystal clear that Moses knew God had called him. He knew God had raised him up and put him in a position of leadership so he could bring deliverance to the Jews. Moses knew God's will for his life but thought it was going to happen by killing an Egyptian. Moses thought the Jews would recognize how God had anointed him to rescue them and deliver them through his position in Pharaoh's household.

We don't know how long Moses had known God's will for his life, but he knew it. Even though Moses knew God was going to use him to deliver the Jews, he totally missed God's timing and plan for bringing it to pass. *This is a critical piece of information for us.* Finding out God's will for our lives is absolutely imperative. *But,* if all we have is knowledge of God's will and aren't sensitive enough to be led by the Holy Spirit, we can blow the whole deal.

Moses blew it big time when he tried to bring God's will to pass in his own strength. His mistake cost him forty years in the wilderness. It also cost the Jews thirty years of extra bondage, which God never intended. We know this because when God made the promise to Abraham, He prophesied that the children of Israel would be sojourners in a foreign land for 400 years (Gen. 15:13)—not 400 years of slavery in Egypt—but a total of 400 years from the time God made the promise. The Israelites were always strangers in the land because they didn't own the land they lived on. The Apostle Paul wrote that the Law came 430 years after the promise (Gal. 3:17). The day Moses led the Israelites out of Egypt was the end of the 430 years (Ex. 12:40).

These calculations don't make you want to jump up, shout, and get all excited, but they are important. It was exactly 430 years from the time of God's prophesy to Abraham, until the children of Israel came out of the land of Egypt—yet God prophesied that it would be 400 years, leaving a 30 year discrepancy. We know that Moses spent 40 years in the wilderness after killing the Egyptian before he encountered God in the burning bush (Acts 7:30). So, if you subtract the 40 years that Moses spent in the wilderness from the 430 years that it took for them to come out of the land of Egypt, they were only in the 390th year of the prophecy when Moses went out and killed the Egyptian and tried to bring God's will to pass. Moses was 10 years premature in trying to bring about what God had put in his heart.

God's will for your life involves His timing. You can't just take a Word from God, make a paragraph out of it, and do whatever you want. God's plans can't be sped up. You can delay God's plan—Moses delayed it forty years—but you can't make it happen any quicker than it's supposed to.

The Bible doesn't tell us exactly what was going on here, but I believe we can guess what Moses was thinking. He was a Jew, who miraculously survived the infanticide of all male Jewish babies in Egypt, and he didn't eke out a living in some remote corner of the world   he grew up in Pharaoh's household! He was raised by Pharaoh's daughter.

Moses was second or third in command over the entire Egyptian nation. Secular accounts say he was a great general who conquered Ethiopia with the military might of Egypt. Moses was a powerful man who had a lot of influence in Egypt. It isn't hard to imagine Moses assuming that it would be his own position and power that would allow him to bring deliverance to the Israelites. But God doesn't rely upon the strength of man.

God wasn't going to deliver Israel in some way that would allow Moses to get all of the credit. It wasn't going to be Moses' position within the household of Pharaoh that gave Israel freedom; God was going to do it in a miraculous way so there would be no mistaking *who* saved them.

Preparation Time Is Never Wasted Time

A lot of people in the body of Christ take the same approach to God's will as Moses did. They may have stumbled upon God's will, but after they know what God wants them to do, they think, *Okay, God, I can handle it from here. You just get me introduced, put me on the stage, and I'll do the rest. Lord, what a wise choice You made in picking me. I can see Your wisdom.* A lot of ministers approach God's will in the same way. God touched them, but now they are trying to build God's kingdom in their own ability, using their own wisdom—this is causing tremendous problems in the body of Christ.

God is going to call you to do something that is absolutely beyond your natural ability. He wants to do things in a supernatural way so it testifies of His glory and people will recognize His love for them. God uses people to do things beyond their ability, so when others see it, they say, "Wow! That had to be God!" God uses the base things of the world, things that are despised, things that are nothing, so no flesh will glory in His presence and say, "Look what I did." (1 Cor. 1:26-30)

God is going to call you to do something that is beyond yourself so you will rely on His power. Then, when people see God's power, they will give Him the glory. God wanted to do something supernatural through Moses, but he initially made the mistake of trying to get it done on his own. No one knows for sure whether Moses knew of the prophecy that said Israel would be delivered after 400 years, but I suspect he did—the Jews were very diligent in passing on their history. I believe Moses knew he was ten years premature.

We are just as eager today to get things done instead of waiting around. We use reasoning to justify our impatience—in violation of Scripture—because it's convenient. The Bible teaches us not to put a novice into a position of leadership (1 Tim 3:6), yet we regularly make newly born-again movie stars, athletes, and politicians the star representatives of Christianity. We do this in order to take advantage of their popularity. We think we can use their clout to promote the Gospel. We don't want to wait, because they might lose their stature during the time it takes them to mature. Such impatience can backfire when the new believer gets lifted up in pride or falls into public scandal because of his or her immaturity.

OUTLINE • 7.1

I.   Moses was a great man of God—he pursued God's will for his life with tremendous dedication, but he also made some major mistake along the way.

   A. He had a revelation of God's will for his life but not a clue how to fulfill it.

   B. God preserved Moses through the time of infanticide in Egypt.

   C. God sent Moses directly to Pharaoh to supply his upbringing, education, and training (Ex. 2:11-15).

   D. Scripture shows that Moses knew his heritage as a Jew:

   In which time Moses was born, and was exceeding fair, and nourished up in his father's house three months: [21] And when he was cast out, Pharaoh's daughter took him up, and nourished him for her own son. [22] And Moses was learned in all the wisdom of the Egyptians, and was mighty in words and in deeds. [23] And when he was full forty years old, it came into his heart to visit his brethren the children of Israel.

   ACTS 7:20-23

   E. Moses didn't "find" himself among the Jews accidentally when he saw the Hebrew man being beaten; it was in his heart to be there.

II.   Timing is everything!

   And seeing one of them suffer wrong, he defended him, and avenged him that was oppressed, and smote the Egyptian: [25] For he supposed his brethren would have understood how that God by his hand would deliver them: but they understood not.

   ACTS 7:24-25

   A. This verse makes it crystal clear that Moses knew God had called him.

   B. He thought the Jews would recognize how God had anointed him to rescue them, but he totally missed God's timing and plan.

   C. This is a critical piece of information.

   D. Finding out God's will for our lives is absolutely imperative.

   E. God's will for our lives involves His timing.

   F. It isn't hard to imagine that Moses assumed it would be his position and power that would allow him to bring deliverance to the Israelites.

   G. But God doesn't rely on the strength of man.

   H. God was going to deliver the Israelites in a miraculous way so there would be no mistaking *who* saved them.

III.   Preparation time is never wasted time.

    A. A lot of people stumble upon God's will and think, *Okay God, I can take it from here.*

    B. Using their own wisdom, they cause tremendous problems in the body of Christ.

    C. God is going to call you to do something that is absolutely beyond your natural ability.

    D. He wants to do things in a supernatural way, so it testifies of His glory and people will recognize His love for them.

    E. Moses initially made the mistake of trying to get it done on his own.

    F. We are just as eager today to get things done instead of waiting around.

        i.   We justify our impatience—in violation of Scripture—because it's convenient.

    G. We make newly born-again movie stars, athletes, and politicians the star representatives of Christianity; we think we can use their clout to promote the Gospel, but it all backfires when they fall.

TEACHER'S GUIDE • 7.1

1. Moses was a great man of God—he pursued God's will for his life with tremendous dedication, but he also made some major mistakes along the way. He had a revelation of God's will for his life but not a clue how to fulfill it. God preserved Moses through the time of infanticide in Egypt, and sent him directly to Pharaoh to supply his upbringing, education, and training (Ex. 2:11-15). Scripture shows that Moses knew his heritage as a Jew:

> *In which time Moses was born, and was exceeding fair, and nourished up in his father's house three months: And when he was cast out, Pharaoh's daughter took him up, and nourished him for her own son. And Moses was learned in all the wisdom of the Egyptians, and was mighty in words and in deeds. And when he was full forty years old, it came into his heart to visit his brethren the children of Israel.*
>
> ACTS 7:20-23

Moses didn't "find" himself among the Jews accidentally when he saw the Hebrew man being beaten; it was in his heart to be there.

1a. It's important to know God's will for your life, but you also need to know what?
     How to fulfill God's will

1b. True or false: According to Acts 7:20-23, it was Moses' idea to visit his brethren, the children of Israel.
     False

2. Timing is everything!

> *And seeing one of them suffer wrong, he defended him, and avenged him that was oppressed, and smote the Egyptian: For he supposed his brethren would have understood how that God by his hand would deliver them: but they understood not.*
>
> ACTS 7:24-25

This verse makes it crystal clear that Moses knew God had called him. He thought the Jews would recognize how God had anointed him to rescue them, but he totally missed God's timing and plan. *This is a critical piece of information for us*—finding out God's will for our lives is absolutely imperative. God's will for our lives involves His timing. It isn't hard to imagine that Moses assumed it would be his position and power that would allow him to bring deliverance to the Israelites. But God doesn't rely on the strength of man. God was going to deliver the Israelites in a miraculous way so there would be no mistaking *who* saved them.

2a. True or false: Even though you can have the anointing of God on your life, you can still miss God's timing and plan.
True

2b. Discussion question: Identify some times and situations in your life that you thought it only logical that the Lord would use your job or social position or status at church (i.e., being on the worship team) to accomplish mighty works. In what has that been true and not true?
Discussion question

2c. God was going to deliver the Israelites in a miraculous way so there would be no _____ who saved them.
Mistaking

3. Preparation time is never wasted time. A lot of people stumble upon God's will and think, *Okay, God, I can take it from here.* By using their own wisdom, they cause tremendous problems in the body of Christ, and actually turn people off of the Gospel. God is going to call you to do something that is absolutely beyond your natural ability. He wants to do things in a supernatural way so it testifies of His glory and people will recognize His love for them. Moses initially made the mistake of trying to get it done on his own. We are just as eager today to get things done instead of waiting around, and we justify our impatience—in violation of Scripture—because it is convenient. We make newly born-again movie stars, athletes, and politicians the star representatives of Christianity; we think we can use their clout to promote the Gospel. But it all backfires when they fall.

3a.　Discussion question: Why do you think preparation time is never wasted time?
　　　Discussion question

3b.　God wants to do things in a supernatural way so it testifies of what?
　　　His glory

3c.　What will people recognize?
　　　A.　His love for them
　　　B.　That He can squash them
　　　C.　A new formula to approach God
　　　D.　All of the above
　　　E.　None of the above
　　　A.　His love for them

3d.　It was a mistake for Moses to initially do what?
　　　Try to get it done on His own

DISCIPLESHIP QUESTIONS • 7.1

1. It's important to know God's will for your life, but you also need to know what?

   _____

   _____

   _____

2. True or false: According to Acts 7:20-23, it was Moses' idea to visit his brethren, the children of Israel.

3. True or false: Even though you can have the anointing of God on your life, you can still miss God's timing and plan.

4. Discussion question: Identify some times and situations in your life that you thought it only logical that the Lord would use your job or social position or status at church (i.e., being on the worship team) to accomplish mighty works. In what has that been true and not true?

   _____

   _____

   _____

5. God was going to deliver the Israelites in a miraculous way so there would be no _____ *who* saved them.

6. Discussion question: Why do you think preparation time is never wasted time?

   _____

   _____

   _____

7. God wants to do things in a supernatural way so it testifies of what?

   _____

   _____

   _____

8. What will people recognize?
   A. His love for them
   B. That He can squash them
   C. A new formula to approach God
   D. All of the above
   E. None of the above

9. It was a mistake for Moses to initially do what?

_____

_____

_____

ANSWER KEY • 7.1

1. How to fulfill God's will
2. False
3. True
4. *Discussion question*
5. Mistaking
6. *Discussion question*
7 His glory
8. A. His love for them
9. Try to get it done on His own

EXODUS 1:15-16

And the king of Egypt spake to the Hebrew midwives, of which the name of the one was Shiphrah, and the name of the other Puah: [16] And he said, When ye do the office of a midwife to the Hebrew women, and see them upon the stools; if it be a son, then ye shall kill him: but if it be a daughter, then she shall live.

MATTHEW 2:16

Then Herod, when he saw that he was mocked of the wise men, was exceeding wroth, and sent forth, and slew all the children that were in Bethlehem, and in all the coasts thereof, from two years old and under, according to the time which he had diligently enquired of the wise men.

EXODUS 2:11-15

And it came to pass in those days, when Moses was grown, that he went out unto his brethren, and looked on their burdens: and he spied an Egyptian smiting an Hebrew, one of his brethren. [12] And he looked this way and that way, and when he saw that there was no man, he slew the Egyptian, and hid him in the sand. [13] And when he went out the second day, behold, two men of the Hebrews strove together: and he said to him that did the wrong, Wherefore smitest thou thy fellow? [14] And he said, Who made thee a prince and a judge over us? intendest thou to kill me, as thou killedst the Egyptian? And Moses feared, and said, Surely this thing is known. [15] Now when Pharaoh heard this thing, he sought to slay Moses. But Moses fled from the face of Pharaoh, and dwelt in the land of Midian: and he sat down by a well.

ACTS 7:20-25

In which time Moses was born, and was exceeding fair, and nourished up in his father's house three months: [21] And when he was cast out, Pharaoh's daughter took him up, and nourished him for her own son. [22] And Moses was learned in all the wisdom of the Egyptians, and was mighty in words and in deeds. [23] And when he was full forty years old, it came into his heart to visit his brethren the children of Israel. [24] And seeing one of them suffer wrong, defended him, and avenged him that was oppressed, and smote the Egyptian: [25] For he supposed his brethren would have understood how that God by his hand would deliver them; but they understood not.

GENESIS 15:13

And he said unto Abram, Know of a surety that thy seed shall be a stranger in a land that is not theirs, and shall serve them; and they shall afflict them four hundred years.

GALATIANS 3:17

And this I say, that the covenant, that was confirmed before of God in Christ, the law, which was four hundred and thirty years after, cannot disannul, that it should make the promise of none effect.

EXODUS 12:40

Now the sojourning of the children of Israel, who dwelt in Egypt, was four hundred and thirty years.

ACTS 7:30

And when forty years were expired, there appeared to him in the wilderness of mount Sina an angel of the Lord in a flame of fire in a bush.

1 CORINTHIANS 1:26-30

For ye see your calling, brethren, how that not many wise men after the flesh, not many mighty, not many noble, are called: [27] But God hath chosen the foolish things of the world to confound the wise; and God hath chosen the weak things of the world to confound the things which are mighty; [28] And base things of the world, and things which are despised, hath God chosen, yea, and things which are not, to bring to nought things that are: [29] That no flesh should glory in his presence. [30] But of him are ye in Christ Jesus, who of God is made unto us wisdom, and righteousness, and sanctification, and redemption.

1 TIMOTHY 3:6

Not a novice, lest being lifted up with pride he fall into the condemnation of the devil.

LESSON 7.2

Moses could have used the same "hurry-up" logic that we use today. Maybe he observed all of the Jews dying under the harsh conditions in Egypt—say it was 100,000 people a year—and he thought, *God, I know it's still ten years before the prophecy will come to pass, but if I don't do something now, one million people are going to die before You deliver them from Egypt.* It's the same logic we use when we let our needs and circumstances motivate us to do things contrary to how God has instructed us. The problem with this logic is that Moses' impatience actually delayed the Israelites' deliverance thirty years, which means that an extra three million people died unnecessarily. God would have brought them out from slavery thirty years earlier if Moses had followed His timing.

This is exactly how we act today. For instance, someone discovers that God has called them to be an evangelist, but they think, *I can't wait—people are dying and going to hell. I can't take time to go to Bible school or get prepared. I have to get out and start reaching people right now!* What he isn't considering is how many people might be turned off to the Lord because he got out there in his own strength and made a mess of things. We can't count how many people will be turned away from God if we crash and become a negative statistic. There is a right way and a wrong way to go about accomplishing God's will.

God revealed His will to Moses ten years before he was supposed to deliver the Jews from Egypt, in order to prepare him for what was ahead. From the time Samuel anointed David to be king, until he actually became king, was a minimum of thirteen years. The Apostle Paul spent fourteen years preparing for his ministry. If you go through the Bible and study the lives of the main characters, you will see that *ten years would have been the least amount of time anybody spent in preparation to be used by God in a major way!* I believe if Moses had waited another ten years, he could have prepared in the luxury of Pharaoh's palace, without all the hardships of the wilderness. God didn't send Moses into the desert. Moses went there for forty years because he committed murder trying to bring God's will to pass in his own strength.

Do It God's Way

The moment most people get any kind of direction from God, *zoom*—they are gone. They don't wait for instructions. It's just as important to understand God's plan for accomplishing His will as it is to discover what His will is. You need the wisdom of God to be able to accomplish His will. He may want you to do something in a way that is totally different from anything you have ever seen before. Too many people in the body of Christ are just copying what other preachers are doing. One church builds a successful ministry by sending buses into poor neighborhoods to give free rides, so everybody starts a "bus ministry." Another pastor starts a "seeker-friendly" church, so everyone goes to a conference to learn how to mimic that approach. God has a plan for *you*, and He can tell *you* what to do. You will only find out what God is leading you to do through a personal relationship with Him.

God's way of doing things is different than our way. For instance, it makes sense from a worldly perspective to hoard money when you are in need, but hoarding is wrong. The Bible teaches us to give and riches will be given unto us. God just does things differently than we do (Is. 55:8-9).

Jesus came upon Peter, James, and John one morning after they had been toiling all night in their fishing boats and hadn't caught a thing (Luke 5). They were gathering up their gear and getting ready to quit. Jesus told them to launch out into the deep and let down their nets one more time. Peter replied, *"Master, we have toiled all the night, and have taken nothing: nevertheless at thy word I will let down the net"* (Luke 5:5). They did the same thing they had been doing the entire previous night, but this time, they did it with God's direction—and every fish in the Sea of Galilee tried to jump into their net! They caught so many fish that the net broke.

Notice that Jesus told them to let down their *nets*, plural, but they only let down *one* net. They obeyed, but they didn't *totally* obey. They half-way obeyed because they weren't expecting much. So, instead of letting down several nets, they only let down one. The single net they put into the sea couldn't contain all of the fish God had for them—so it broke. Many of the fish must have escaped. Think of the haul they would have had if they had completely obeyed Jesus by putting down multiple nets.

As you allow God to lead you, you might feel led to do something you have already done in the past. Don't immediately think, *Oh, I've already tried this and it didn't work.* Maybe it didn't work because you were trying to do it on your own instead of at God's command. You might do the exact same thing you did before and get totally different results because you would be doing it under God's anointing and leadership this time.

God doesn't have a "one-size-fits-all" approach for building His kingdom. Our personal relationship with Jesus allows Him to guide us individually. It is one of the things that sets Christianity apart from every other religion on the face of the earth. Other religions have systems and rules and regulations, but we have a personal relationship. Every believer is God-possessed. Jesus lives on the inside of us. The Holy Spirit comes and fills us. He will talk to us, teach us, and guide us. He doesn't only speak to preachers and full-time ministers; the Holy Spirit is available to every born-again believer.

Moses had a word from God, but he didn't follow God's timing. Moses did what most of us would have done: He went out on his own and blew it. *We are not capable of representing God and accomplishing His plans in our own strength and ability.* The Lord didn't create us to be wound up like a toy robot so He could release us to go off on our own speed and energy. We have to be God dependent. One of my favorite scriptures is, *"O LORD, I know that the way of man is not in himself: it is not in man that walketh to direct his steps"* (Jer. 10:23). We not only need to find God's will; we need to find His timing and plan for accomplishing it—which is only going to come through a relationship with the Lord that is built upon prayer and studying the Word.

IV. Moses may have observed all the Jews dying under harsh conditions in Egypt and thought, *If I don't do something now, a million people are going to die.*

  A. That's the same logic we use when we let our needs and circumstances motivate us to do things contrary to how God has instructed us.

  B. Moses' impatience delayed the Israelites' deliverance thirty years.

  C. This is exactly how we act today—*I can't wait—people are dying and going to hell. I can't take time to go to Bible school or get prepared. I have to get out and start reaching people right now!*

  D. There is a right way and a wrong way to go about accomplishing God's will.

  E. God revealed His will to Moses ten years before he was supposed to deliver the Jews from Egypt to prepare him for what was ahead.

  F. Throughout the Bible, *ten years would have been the least amount of time anybody spent in preparation to be used by God in a major way!*

  G. God didn't send Moses into the desert; he went there because he committed murder trying to bring God's will to pass in his own strength.

V. Do it God's way.

  A. The moment most people get any kind of direction from God, *zoom*—they are gone!

  B. You need the wisdom of God to be able to accomplish his will.

  C. God may want you to do something in a way that is totally different from anything you have ever seen before.

  D. Too many people copy other preachers.

  E. God has a plan for *you.*

  F. You'll only find out what God's leading you to do through personal relationship with Him.

VI. God's way of doing things is different than your way (Is. 55:8-9).

  A. From a worldly perspective, it makes sense to hoard when you are in need, but the Bible teaches to give.

  B. Under God's anointing and leadership, everything is different.

  C. God doesn't have a "one-size-fits-all" approach for building His kingdom.

D. Other religions have systems, rules, and regulations; Christians have personal relationship.

E. Every believer is God-possessed.

F. The Holy Spirit will talk to you, teach you, and guide you.

O LORD, I know that the way of man is not in himself: it is not in man that walketh to direct his steps.

JEREMIAH 10:23

TEACHER'S GUIDE • 7.2

4. Moses may have observed all the Jews dying under harsh conditions in Egypt and thought, *If I don't do something now, a million people are going to die.* That's the same logic we use when we let our needs and circumstances motivate us to do things contrary to how God has instructed us. Moses' impatience delayed the Israelites' deliverance thirty years. This is exactly how we act today—*I can't wait—people are dying and going to hell. I can't take time to go to Bible school or get prepared. I have to get out and start reaching people right now!* There is a right way and a wrong way to go about accomplishing God's will. God revealed His will to Moses ten years before he was supposed to deliver the Jews from Egypt to prepare him for what was ahead. Throughout the Bible, *ten years would have been the least amount of time anybody spent in preparation to be used by God in a major way!* God didn't send Moses into the desert; he went there because he committed murder trying to bring God's will to pass in his own strength.

4a. Discussion question: When people see suffering, they often experience an intense desire to help, which can cause them to skip the right amount of preparation. What are some current situations that put this pressure on your emotions? How you are dealing with it? What are you currently doing to prepare for future work?
Discussion question

5. Do it God's way. The moment most people get any kind of direction from God, *zoom*—they are gone! You need the wisdom of God to be able to accomplish his will. God may want you to do something in a way that is totally different from anything you have ever seen before. Too many people copy other preachers. God has a plan for *you*. You'll only find out what God's leading you to do through personal relationship with Him.

5a. Why would it be wrong to copy what other ministries have done?
   A. Even though you might succeed, no one will remember you if you are not unique
   B. Copycats are a stink in God's nostrils
   C. God may want you to do something in a way that is totally different from anything you have ever seen before
   D. All of the above
   E. None of the above
   C. God may want you to do something in a way that is totally different from anything you have ever seen before

5b. How do you find out what God is leading you to do?
   A. Asking your neighbor
   B. Praying and going to communion
   C. Living holy
   D. Through personal relationship with Him
   E. Praying in tongues at the same time every day
   D. Through personal relationship with Him

5c. True or false: "Doing things "God's way," according to His specific plan for you, means that every morning when you get up, you need to ask Him which side of the toast to butter.
   False

6. God's way of doing things is different than your way (Is. 55:8-9). From a worldly perspective, it makes sense to hoard when you are in need, but the Bible teaches to give. Under God's anointing and leadership, everything is different. God doesn't have a "one-size-fits-all" approach for building His kingdom. Other religions have systems, rules, and regulations; Christians have personal relationship. Every believer is God-possessed. The Holy Spirit will talk to you, teach you, and guide you.

> O LORD, I know that the way of man is not in himself: it is not in man that walketh to direct his steps.
>
> JEREMIAH 10:23

6a. True or false: According to Isaiah 55:8-9, God's ways are not the same as man's.
True

6b. How is Christianity set apart from every other religions?
   A. Because it doesn't have as many rules and regulations
   B. Because it's all about reincarnation
   C. Because it has water baptism
   D. Because you have a personal relationship with God
   E. Because it appeals to your sensibilities
   D. Because you have a personal relationship with God

6c. Discussion question: Why does Jeremiah 10:23 apply to believers as well as unbelievers?
Discussion question

10. Discussion question: When people see suffering, they often experience an intense desire to help, which can cause them to skip the right amount of preparation. What are some current situations that put this pressure on your emotions? How you are dealing with it? What are you currently doing to prepare for future work?

_____

_____

_____

11. Why would it be wrong to copy what other ministries have done?
    A. Even though you might succeed, no one will remember you if you are not unique
    B. Copycats are a stink in God's nostrils
    C. God may want you to do something in a way that is totally different from anything you have ever seen before
    D. All of the above
    E. None of the above

12. How do you find out what God is leading you to do?
    A. Asking your neighbor
    B. Praying and going to communion
    C. Living holy
    D. Through personal relationship with Him
    E. Praying in tongues at the same time every day

_____

_____

_____

13. True or false: "Doing things "God's way," according to His specific plan for you, means that every morning when you get up, you need to ask Him which side of the toast to butter.

14. True or false: According to Isaiah 55:8-9, God's ways are not the same as man's.

15. How is Christianity set apart from every other religions?
    A. Because it doesn't have as many rules and regulations
    B. Because it's all about reincarnation
    C. Because it has water baptism
    D. Because you have a personal relationship with God
    E. Because it appeals to your sensibilities

16. Discussion question: Why does Jeremiah 10:23 apply to believers as well as unbelievers?

_____

_____

_____

ANSWER KEY • 7.2

10. *Discussion question*
11. C.   God may want you to do something in a way that is totally different from anything you have ever seen before
12. D.   Through personal relationship with Him
13. False
14. True
15. D.   Because you have a personal relationship with God
16. *Discussion question*

ISAIAH 55:8-9

For my thoughts are not your thoughts, neither are your ways my ways, saith the Lord. [9] For as the heavens are higher than the earth, so are my ways higher than your ways, and my thoughts than your thoughts.

LUKE 5:5

And Simon answering said unto him, Master, we have toiled all the night, and have taken nothing: nevertheless at thy word I will let down the net.

JEREMIAH 10:23

O Lord, I know that the way of man is not in himself: it is not man that walketh to direct his steps.

IT TAKES EFFORT

LESSON 8.1

Moses blew it when he killed the Egyptian, but he recovered and eventually went on to accomplish God's will. He spent forty years in the wilderness praying and asking God for another chance. He knew God had a plan for his life. He never stopped seeking after God and trying to fulfill his purpose. Moses was actively looking for God. So, when he saw a bush that was burning but wasn't being consumed by the flames, he turned aside to investigate.

> *Now Moses kept the flock of Jethro his father in law, the priest of Midian: and he led the flock to the backside of the desert, and came to the mountain of God, even to Horeb. [2] And the angel of the LORD appeared unto him in a flame of fire out of the midst of a bush: and he looked, and, behold, the bush burned with fire, and the bush was not consumed. [3] And Moses said, I will now turn aside, and see this great sight, why the bush is not burnt. [4] And when the LORD saw that he turned aside to see, God called unto him out of the midst of the bush, and said, Moses, Moses. And he said, Here am I.*
>
> EXODUS 3:1-4

It was only after Moses turned aside to check things out that the voice of God came to him. Moses could have walked right by the burning bush. He could have been focused on how far he had to travel with the flock. He could have been anxious to get them water by a certain time. I'm sure he was busy, but he was still looking for God. Then when he saw something abnormal, he stopped to investigate.

This same thing happened to the disciples when they were in the boat, struggling to survive a storm in the middle of the Sea of Galilee. Jesus came walking to them on the water. The Scripture says He would have passed them by (Mark 6:48). Jesus was there to save His disciples. He wasn't out on the lake for a stroll and just so happened to walk close to their boat. No, Jesus was there to help them. But this is how God operates: He delights in faith. We have to be looking for Him.

God makes His presence known, but He isn't going to force anyone to pay attention. God doesn't come into our lives and *make* us follow Him. To Moses' credit, he persevered in looking for God. He believed that God was still going to use him (Heb. 11:27). If Moses had not turned aside to inspect the burning bush, it's very possible God wouldn't have spoken to him.

It's our hardheartedness that makes us so insensitive to God. He isn't hard to find; it's just that most of us are looking in the wrong places. We are occupied with the wrong things. The Bible says when we seek, we find. We can't say, "God, if You can reach me in the next five minutes, before my favorite television program comes on, I'll serve You for the rest of my life." God doesn't work on our timetable. We have to seek Him with all of our hearts (Jer. 29:13), expecting to see Him intervene.

And he said, Draw not nigh hither: put off thy shoes from off thy feet, for the place whereon thou standest is holy ground. [6] Moreover he said, I am the God of thy father, the God of Abraham, the God of Isaac, and the God of Jacob. And Moses hid his face; for he was afraid to look upon God.

EXODUS 3:5-6

The Lord went on to tell Moses that He was sending him down to Egypt to bring the Israelites out. Moses replied, *"Who am I, that I should go unto Pharaoh, and that I should bring forth the children of Israel out of Egypt?"* (Ex. 3:11).

Moses responded to God by saying, "I can't talk. I'm not wise. I'm not learned. They won't listen to me." Yet Moses was educated in all of the wisdom of the Egyptians and was mighty in word and deed (Acts 7:22). The Egyptians were a very advanced society, so Moses wasn't a fool. He was wise. Moses was just like you and me when we say we can't do something God asks us to do. The truth is, we can do it, but we get intimidated or overwhelmed so we start saying that we can't. With God's help and His anointing, we can do anything He asks us to (Phil. 4:13).

This attitude is in stark contrast to Moses' self-confidence forty years earlier. It took a few decades in the wilderness for Moses to come to the end of himself. As long as you are sufficient in yourself—trusting in yourself—then you are going to have a hard time trusting God. You won't find the beginning of God until you get to the end of yourself. Moses was a different person with a different outlook. He was no longer second-in-command over all of Egypt—he was working for his father-in-law, herding sheep on the back side of the desert. Moses had lost the arrogance and self-will from his days as a prince of the world.

The Rod of God

Moses was looking for an opportunity to get back and fulfill God's will, yet he had lost his self-confidence. He still believed God was going to use him, but he had to realize he couldn't do it on his own. Moses told the Lord he couldn't do it and that the people wouldn't believe him.

> And the LORD said unto him, What is that in thine hand? And he said, A rod. *[3]* And he said, Cast it on the ground. And he cast it on the ground, and it became a serpent; and Moses fled from before it. *[4]* And the LORD said unto Moses, Put forth thine hand, and take it by the tail. And he put forth his hand, and caught it, and it became a rod in his hand.
>
> EXODUS 4:2-4

Moses fled from the snake in fear. God called him back and told him to pick it up by the tail. Picking up a serpent by the tail means you have no control. In order to control a snake, you have to grab it right behind the jaws; otherwise, it can turn and bite you. Moses was putting his life on the line by grabbing the tail of a venomous snake, which shows that he was willing to risk death in order to obey God.

Moses had been in "Bush University" for forty years, and this was his final exam. Would he pass or fail? When God told Moses to pick up the snake by the tail, He was saying, "Show Me that you are willing to do it My way." This would show that he was no longer dependent on his own understanding. Moses picked up the snake by the tail, thinking it was going to kill him, but instead the snake turned back into a stick. After all he had been through, Moses finally understood that God's way was better.

The Lord has to accomplish this same thing in everyone. All of us tend to want to control our own lives. We don't like being told what to do—not even by God. It's a characteristic of fallen human beings to want to do things our own way. In the process of finding God's will and trying to fulfill it, sooner or later, we are going to think that we know more than He does. He has to get us to the place where we are no longer running the show but, rather, deferring to His wisdom.

> And Moses took his wife and his sons, and set them upon an ass, and he returned to the land of Egypt: and Moses took the rod of God in his hand.
>
> EXODUS 4:20

When Moses approached the burning bush, God asked him what he held in his hand. Moses answered that he was holding a stick. It was a plain old stick that Moses threw down before God, but when God gave it back to him, the Bible calls it *"the rod of God."* It wasn't Moses' stick anymore. It was God's stick. This is what God is asking of every believer. If you want to follow God's will, you will go through a process like this—where God is going to ask "Will you really trust me?" He is going to ask you to sacrifice something. He will ask you to lay down your life and turn it over to Him. If you keep control of your own life, it will never have any more power than what you can put behind it. By becoming a living sacrifice and turning your life over to God, you will gain God's strength.

Moses received much more in return than he gave. He gave up a stick, a dead piece of wood, and God gave him back something that turned a river into blood, parted a sea, caused hail to fall out of a clear sky, and water to gush from a rock. Moses received the power of God! You will always come out on top when you make a trade with God. God may ask for everything you have, but He will give you everything He has in return. You will always be better off when lay your life down for God.

OUTLINE • 8.1

I. Moses blew it when he killed the Egyptian, but he recovered and eventually went on to accomplish God's will.

   A. He never stopped seeking after God and trying to fulfill his purpose.

   B. So, when he saw a bush that was burning but wasn't being consumed by the flames, he turned aside to investigate.

   Now Moses kept the flock of Jethro his father in law, the priest of Midian: and he led the flock to the backside of the desert, and came to the mountain of God, even to Horeb. [2] And the angel of the Lord appeared unto him in a flame of fire out of the midst of a bush: and he looked, and, behold, the bush burned with fire, and the bush was not consumed. [3] And Moses said, I will now turn aside, and see this great sight, why the bush is not burnt. [4] And when the Lord saw that he turned aside to see, God called unto him out of the midst of the bush, and said, Moses, Moses. And he said, Here am I.

   EXODUS 3:1-4

   C. It was only after Moses turned aside to check things out that the voice of God came to him.

   D. This is how God operates: He delights in faith—we have to be looking for Him.

   E. If Moses had not turned aside to inspect the burning bush, it's very possible God wouldn't have spoken to him.

   F. God isn't hard to find; it's just that most of us are looking in the wrong places.

   G. We have to seek Him with all of our hearts (Jer. 29:13), expecting to see Him intervene.

   H. The truth is, we can do what God asks us to do, but we get intimidated or overwhelmed so we start saying that we can't.

   I. With God's help and His anointing, we can do anything He asks us to (Phil. 4:13).

   J. We won't find the beginning of God until we get to the end of ourselves.

II. Moses was looking for an opportunity to get back and fulfill God's will, yet he had lost his self-confidence.

   A. He still believed God was going to use him, but he had to realize he couldn't do it on his own.

   And the Lord said unto him, What is that in thine hand? And he said, A rod. [3] And he said, Cast it on the ground. And he cast it on the ground, and it became a serpent; and Moses fled from before it. [4] And the Lord said unto Moses, Put forth thine hand, and take it by the tail. And he put forth his hand, and caught it, and it became a rod in his hand.

   EXODUS 4:2-4

B. God called Moses back and told him to pick the snake up by the tail.

C. Picking up a serpent by the tail means you have no control.

D. When God told Moses to pick up the snake by the tail, He was saying, "Show Me that you are willing to do it My way."

E. It's a characteristic of fallen human beings to want to do things their own way.

F. He has to get you to the place where you are no longer running the show but, rather, deferring to His wisdom.

G. If you keep control of your own life, it will never have any more power than what you can put behind it.

H. By becoming a living sacrifice and turning your life over to God, you will gain God's strength.

I. God may ask for everything you have, but He will give you everything He has in return.

1. Moses blew it when he killed the Egyptian, but he recovered and eventually went on to accomplish God's will. He never stopped seeking after God and trying to fulfill his purpose. So, when he saw a bush that was burning but wasn't being consumed by the flames, he turned aside to investigate.

> *Now Moses kept the flock of Jethro his father in law, the priest of Midian: and he led the flock to the backside of the desert, and came to the mountain of God, even to Horeb. [2] And the angel of the LORD appeared unto him in a flame of fire out of the midst of a bush: and he looked, and, behold, the bush burned with fire, and the bush was not consumed. [3] And Moses said, I will now turn aside, and see this great sight, why the bush is not burnt. [4] And when the LORD saw that he turned aside to see, God called unto him out of the midst of the bush, and said, Moses, Moses. And he said, Here am I.*
>
> EXODUS 3:1-4

It was only after Moses turned aside to check things out that the voice of God came to him. This is how God operates: He delights in faith—we have to be looking for Him. If Moses had not turned aside to inspect the burning bush, it's very possible God wouldn't have spoken to him. God isn't hard to find; it's just that most of us are looking in the wrong places. We have to seek Him with all of our hearts (Jer. 29:13), expecting to see Him intervene. The truth is, we can do what God asks us to do, but we get intimidated or overwhelmed so we start saying that we can't. With God's help and His anointing, we can do anything He asks us to (Phil. 4:13). We won't find the beginning of God until we get to the end of ourselves.

1a.　You have to be _____ for God.
　　　A. Looking
　　　B. Working
　　　C. Stealing
　　　D. All of the above
　　　E. None of the above
　　　A. Looking

1b.　Which scripture tells you that you have to seek God with all of your heart?
　　　Jeremiah 29:13

1c.　Discussion question: Are there any areas of your life where you have been intimidated or overwhelmed by what God has asked you to do that you have said you can't? If so, how do you plan to handle this?
　　　Discussion question

1d.　Discussion question: What does "you won't find the beginning of God until you get to the end of yourself" mean to you?
　　　Discussion question

2. Moses was looking for an opportunity to get back and fulfill God's will, yet he had lost his self-confidence. He still believed God was going to use him, but he had to realize he couldn't do it on his own.

> *And the LORD said unto him, What is that in thine hand? And he said, A rod. [3] And he said, Cast it on the ground. And he cast it on the ground, and it became a serpent; and Moses fled from before it. [4] And the LORD said unto Moses, Put forth thine hand, and take it by the tail. And he put forth his hand, and caught it, and it became a rod in his hand.*
>
> EXODUS 4:2-4

God called Moses back and told him to pick the snake up by the tail. Picking up a serpent by the tail means you have no control. When God told Moses to pick up the snake by the tail, He was saying, "Show Me that you are willing to do it My way." It's a characteristic of fallen human beings to want to do things their own way. He has to get you to the place where you are no longer running the show but, rather, deferring to His wisdom. If you keep control of your own life, it will never have any more power than what you can put behind it. By becoming a living sacrifice and turning your life over to God, you will gain God's strength. God may ask for everything you have, but He will give you everything He has in return.

2a. What did Moses have to realize?
   That he couldn't do it on his own

2b. True or false: Picking up a serpent by the tail means you have total control.
   False

2c. Discussion question: Have you experienced God asking you for something you have and giving you something in return? In what way?
   Discussion question

DISCIPLESHIP QUESTIONS • 8.1

1. You have to be _____ for God.
   A. Looking
   B. Working
   C. Stealing
   D. All of the above
   E. None of the above

2. Which scripture tells you that you have to seek God with all of your heart?

   _____

   _____

   _____

3. Discussion question: Are there any areas of your life where you have been intimidated or overwhelmed by what God has asked you to do that you have said you can't? If so, how do you plan to handle this?

   _____

   _____

   _____

4. Discussion question: What does "you won't find the beginning of God until you get to the end of yourself" mean to you?

   _____

   _____

   _____

5. What did Moses have to realize?

   _____

   _____

   _____

6. True or false: Picking up a serpent by the tail means you have total control.

7. Discussion question: Have you experienced God asking you for something you have and giving you something in return? In what way?

_____

_____

_____

ANSWER KEY • 8.1

1. A. Looking
2. Jeremiah 29:13
3. *Discussion question*
4. *Discussion question*
5. That he couldn't do it on his own
6. False
7. *Discussion question*

EXODUS 3:1-6

Now Moses kept the flock of Jethro his father in law, the priest of Midian: and he led the flock to the backside of the desert, and came to the mountain of God, even to Horeb. [2] And the angel of the LORD appeared unto him in a flame of fire out of the midst of a bush: and he looked, and, behold, the bush burned with fire, and the bush was not consumed. [3] And Moses said, I will now turn aside, and see this great sight, why the bush is not burnt. [4] And when the LORD saw that he turned aside to see, God called unto him out of the midst of the bush, and said, Moses, Moses. And he said, Here am I. [5] And he said, Draw not nigh hither: put off thy shoes from off thy feet, for the place whereon thou standest is holy ground. [6] Moreover he said, I am the God of thy father, the God of Abraham, the God of Isaac, and the God of Jacob. And Moses hid his face; for he was afraid to look upon God.

MARK 6:48

And he saw them toiling in rowing; for the wind was contrary unto them: and about the fourth watch of the night he cometh unto them, walking upon the sea, and would have passed by them.

HEBREWS 11:27

By faith he forsook Egypt, not fearing the wrath of the king: for he endured, as seeing him who is invisible.

JEREMIAH 29:13

And ye shall seek me, and find me, when ye shall search for me with all your heart.

EXODUS 3:11

And Moses said unto God, Who am I, that I should go unto Pharaoh, and that I should bring forth the children of Israel out of Egypt?

ACTS 7:22

And Moses was learned in all the wisdom of the Egyptians, and was mighty in words and in deeds.

PHILIPPIANS 4:13

I can do all things through Christ which strengtheneth me.

EXODUS 4:2-4

And the LORD said unto him, What is that in thine hand? And he said, A rod. [3] And he said, Cast it on the ground. And he cast it on the ground, and it became a serpent; and Moses fled from before it. [4] And the LORD said unto Moses, Put forth thine hand, and take it by the tail. And he put forth his hand, and caught it, and it became a rod in his hand.

EXODUS 4:20

And Moses took his wife and his sons, and set them upon an ass, and he returned to the land of Egypt: and Moses took the rod of God in his hand.

LESSON 8.2

One of the things that really helped me when I started following the Lord was ministering in nursing homes. I ministered two or three times a week. This was really good for me because I encountered people who were once very wealthy or successful in life, but the benefit of those things eluded them in old age. I don't believe we have to be decrepit and sick when we grow old, but old age is going to catch up with us. We are going to pass our prime someday.

Unless Jesus comes, every one of us is going to come to the end of our physical strength. The truth is that it doesn't take near that long before most of us crash and burn. We just need to recognize that we cannot accomplish God's will in our own strength and power. So, when God asks us to make a total surrender and yield to Him—whatever He wants us to do—we just need to do it. Then we'll get His strength and power and be much better off.

Christ in You

Is not this the word that we did tell thee in Egypt, saying, Let us alone, that we may serve the Egyptians? For it had been better for us to serve the Egyptians, than that we should die in the wilderness. [13] And Moses said unto the people, Fear ye not, stand still, and see the salvation of the LORD, which he will shew to you to day: for the Egyptians whom ye have seen to day, ye shall see them again no more for ever. [14] The LORD shall fight for you, and ye shall hold your peace.
EXODUS 14:12-14

The Israelites had just left Egypt. They were camped in a valley with mountains on both sides of them, the Red Sea in front of them, and Pharaoh's army coming up behind them. It looked like they were trapped with nowhere to go, yet God instructed Moses to camp there. God hardened Pharaoh's heart to believe that the Israelites were entangled in the land. Pharaoh saw the situation as an opportunity to get revenge against Israel for the plagues and humiliation that God had brought upon Egypt. Basically, the Lord set a trap for Pharaoh. God told Moses what was going to happen, but the people were in full-scale revolt. In a panic, they said, "Why did you bring us out here to die? We should have stayed in Egypt." The situation didn't look promising from a logical standpoint.

The anointing of God came through Moses, and he quieted them by saying, *"Stand still, and see the salvation of the LORD."* He told them they wouldn't have to fight—God was going to fight for them. All of a sudden, the revolt stopped. They were completely silent. Moses had stopped the uprising. But the Egyptians were still coming.

> *And the LORD said unto Moses, Wherefore criest thou unto me? speak unto the children of Israel, that they go forward: [16] But lift thou up thy rod, and stretch out thine hand over the sea, and divide it: and the children of Israel shall go on dry ground through the midst of the sea.*
>
> EXODUS 14:15-16

Somewhere in between Moses' bold statement to the Israelites and what the Lord said here, Moses apparently began to cry out, "God, what are we going to do?" He was asking God to do a miracle—to do something to stop the Egyptians. This seemed reasonable given the situation, but God said, "Why are you crying to Me? Take the rod, hold it out over the sea, and part the sea." Basically the Lord was saying, "Don't you remember that you turned your life over to Me when you picked up the serpent by the tail? That's not your stick you're holding; it's My rod. Now take the authority I have given you and use it." This is a word for us today: Our lives are not our own, Christ lives through us, and we need to use the power He has given us to improve our situation (Gal. 2:20).

Instead of praying for God to do something when we get into crisis situations, we need to recognize that we have the power of God living on the inside of us. Once we have turned our lives over to God, we have power over our circumstances. Cancer, illness, and every kind of lack should tremble in our presence. We need to quit begging God to do something, as if He hasn't done anything. God gave us power. We turned our lives over to Him, so now we need to take the power He gave back to us and command our situations to change. We need to use our God-given authority to do something about our problems.

God told Moses, "Get up off your face, take the rod, and do something." I am convinced that if Moses had stayed there begging and pleading with God, they would all have been destroyed. Prayer has its place, but there comes a time when you have to get up off your knees and do something—a time to believe God's Word and accept that He has given you power and authority to change your circumstances. Use your authority: Command sickness to flee and order the devil to get out of your life. You can't ask God to rebuke the devil for you. He told you to resist the devil to make him flee (James 4:7). You have to be bold.

Trusting God in all circumstances comes from having a deep relationship with Him. You won't fully trust God until you have made yourself a living sacrifice and have seen Him come through for you. Believers should recognize that it is no longer they who live, but Christ living in them (Gal. 2:20). You won't have the boldness to fight against the wiles of the Enemy unless you know that Christ lives in you. Once you have turned your life over to the Lord, you need to use the authority He has given you in exchange so you won't be overcome when the Enemy comes against you in the wilderness.

It's true that you can't accomplish God's will in your own strength, but you have to balance that with the fact that you can do all things through Christ who strengthens you (Phil. 4:13). You need both sides of the equation in balance. Without Christ, I can do nothing, but praise God, I'm not without Christ! God will never leave you nor forsake you (Heb. 13:5). Place no confidence in yourself; have great confidence in Christ, who lives in you. Confidence in God and humility are not opposing truths—they are two sides of the same coin. You need both perspectives to enjoy a healthy relationship with God and walk in victory.

Moses Strikes the Rock

The children of Israel spent forty years in the wilderness. During that time, there was an instance when God had Moses strike a rock with his rod and enough water flowed out of the rock to satisfy 3 million Jews—plus all of their animals (Ex. 17:6). It was absolutely miraculous. Toward the end of the forty years, the people were without water again, but this time, the Lord told Moses to speak to the rock instead of striking it (Num. 20:8). Moses went before the people, stood before the rock, and began to rebuke the people for complaining. Then Moses took his rod and struck the rock, but nothing happened—because God told him to speak to it, not hit it. So, Moses struck the rock a second time, and water gushed out. But the Lord told Moses that he would not live to enter into the Promised Land because of his disobedience in striking the rock (Num. 20:10-12).

By that time, Moses had spent 120 years following God. All Moses did was hit the rock, yet God refused to allow him to enter into the Promised Land. I always heard this scripture explained that the rock symbolized Christ (1 Cor. 10:4), so when Moses hit the rock a second time, it was like trying to crucify Christ twice. In essence, Moses broke the symbolism God was trying to establish by showing that Christ, once crucified, cannot be crucified again (Heb. 6:6). I can see the logic behind this teaching, but it seems harsh to me that God would make Moses miss his entire life's goal just because he broke a symbolic meaning.

I believe the real issue here was Moses' self-will. He had taken things into his own hands once before when he killed the Egyptian, and it cost the children of Israel thirty years of extra bondage. After forty years of leading the people through the wilderness, his self-will was beginning to rise up again. God told him to speak to the rock, but Moses thought it would be more dramatic to hit it. He was exerting his own wisdom and trying to do things his own way again. If God had failed to deal with Moses' self-will, the entire nation of Israel could have spent another forty years in the wilderness. It wasn't just symbolism. God did this to protect Israel from Moses.

We don't ever learn the lesson of humility completely. It's not like we have one encounter with the Lord and then never again have to deal with leaning on our own understanding or ability. Moses laid his life down at the burning bush, but here, he was veering back toward self-reliance. God had to bring Moses back to his dependence on Him.

Some people think everything in the Christian life is supposed to work perfectly after they believe, but it doesn't happen that way. *God uses you in spite of who you are, not because of who you are.* Don't be upset if you believe for perfect health and then get a cold that ruins your record. You will still get over it in two days instead of two weeks. It's no big deal. It doesn't mean that God failed you. It just means that you are growing. You will never do anything perfectly. Perfectionism immobilizes people with anxiety, because they are constantly worried about something going wrong. It makes people so cautious that they never get anything accomplished. People who change the world are people who aren't afraid to step out and take action.

We can learn a few lessons at Moses' expense. Instead of spending forty years in the desert with scorpions and snakes, we can take these teachings to heart and make a decision that will change our lives. We don't have to be wrung out in order for God to use us. If that's your experience, praise God, whatever it takes—but it doesn't have to be that way. The Holy Spirit can teach us by revelation that God's ways are better than our own plans. We need to lay our lives down before God—give Him control. God will take our offering and give us back His life and power in return.

OUTLINE • 8.2

III. Unless Jesus comes, every one of us is going to come to the end of our physical strength.

  A. We just need to recognize that we cannot accomplish God's will in our own strength and power.

  B. So, when God asks us to make a total surrender and yield to Him—whatever He wants us to do—we just need to do it.

  C. Then we'll get His strength and power and be much better off.

IV. The Israelites had just left Egypt, and they were camped in a valley with mountains on both sides of them, the Red Sea in front of them, and Pharaoh's army coming up behind them.

> *Is not this the word that we did tell thee in Egypt, saying, Let us alone, that we may serve the Egyptians? For it had been better for us to serve the Egyptians, than that we should die in the wilderness. [13] And Moses said unto the people, Fear ye not, stand still, and see the salvation of the Lord, which he will shew to you to day: for the Egyptians whom ye have seen to day, ye shall see them again no more for ever. [14] The Lord shall fight for you, and ye shall hold your peace.*
> EXODUS 14:12-14

  A. The situation didn't look promising from a logical standpoint.

  B. Moses was asking God to do a miracle—to do something to stop the Egyptians.

  C. This seemed reasonable given the situation, but God said, "Why are you crying unto Me? Take the rod, hold it out over the sea, and part the sea."

> *And the Lord said unto Moses, Wherefore criest thou unto me? speak unto the children of Israel, that they go forward: [16] But lift thou up thy rod, and stretch out thine hand over the sea, and divide it: and the children of Israel shall go on dry ground through the midst of the sea.*
> EXODUS 14:15-16

  D. Basically the Lord was saying, "Take the authority I have given you and use it."

  E. This is a word for us today: Our lives are not our own, Christ lives through us, and we need to use the power He has given us to improve our situation (Gal. 2:20).

  F. It's true that we can't accomplish God's will in our own strength, but we have to balance that with the fact that we can do all things through Christ who strengthens us (Phil. 4:13).

  G. Without Christ, I can do nothing, but praise God, I'm not without Christ (Heb. 13:5)!

V. Toward the end of their forty years in the wilderness, the Israelites were without water for a second time (Ex. 17:6).

A. This time, the Lord told Moses to speak to the rock instead of striking it (Num. 20:8), but Moses struck the rock twice instead.

B. The Lord told Moses that he would not live to enter into the Promised Land because of his disobedience in striking the rock (Num. 20:10-12).

C. I believe the real issue here was Moses' self-will.

    i. God told him to speak to the rock, but Moses thought it would be more dramatic to hit it.

    ii. He was exerting his own wisdom and trying to do things his own way again.

D. If God had failed to deal with Moses' self-will, the entire nation of Israel could have spent another forty years in the wilderness—God did this to protect Israel from Moses.

E. We don't ever learn the lesson of humility completely: It's not like we have one encounter with the Lord and then never again have to deal with leaning on our own understanding or ability.

F. Some people think everything in the Christian life is supposed to work perfectly after they believe, but it doesn't happen that way.

G. *God uses us in spite of who we are, not because of who we are.*

H. We need to lay our lives down before God—give Him control.

I. God will take our offering and give us back His life and power in return.

3. Unless Jesus comes, every one of us is going to come to the end of our physical strength. We just need to recognize that we cannot accomplish God's will in our own strength and power. So, when God asks us to make a total surrender and yield to Him—whatever He wants us to do—we just need to do it. Then we'll get His strength and power and be much better off.

3a. What do you need to recognize?
   That you cannot accomplish God's will in your own strength

3b. Discussion question: What does it mean to make a total surrender to God and yield to Him?
   Discussion question

4. The Israelites had just left Egypt, and they were camped in a valley with mountains on both sides of them, the Red Sea in front of them, and Pharaoh's army coming up behind them.

> *Is not this the word that we did tell thee in Egypt, saying, Let us alone, that we may serve the Egyptians? For it had been better for us to serve the Egyptians, than that we should die in the wilderness. [13] And Moses said unto the people, Fear ye not, stand still, and see the salvation of the LORD, which he will shew to you to day: for the Egyptians whom ye have seen to day, ye shall see them again no more for ever. [14] The LORD shall fight for you, and ye shall hold your peace.*
>
> EXODUS 14:12-14

The situation didn't look promising from a logical standpoint. Moses was asking God to do a miracle—to do something to stop the Egyptians. This seemed reasonable given the situation, but God said, "Why are you crying unto Me? Take the rod, hold it out over the sea, and part the sea."

> *And the LORD said unto Moses, Wherefore criest thou unto me? speak unto the children of Israel, that they go forward: [16] But lift thou up thy rod, and stretch out thine hand over the sea, and divide it: and the children of Israel shall go on dry ground through the midst of the sea.*
>
> EXODUS 14:15-16

Basically the Lord was saying, "Take the authority I have given you and use it." This is a word for us today: Our lives are not our own, Christ lives through us, and we need to use the power He has given us to improve our situation (Gal. 2:20). It's true that we can't accomplish God's will in our own strength, but we have to balance that with the fact that we can do all things through Christ who strengthens us (Phil. 4:13). Without Christ, I can do nothing, but praise God, I'm not without Christ (Heb. 13:5)!

4a. True or false: The Lord told Moses that He would take care of everything and that Moses didn't have to do anything.
False

4b. Discussion question: In what ways can you live out the ideas that your life is not your own, Christ lives through you, and you need to use the power He has given you to improve your situation (Gal. 2:20)?
Discussion question

4c. Without Christ, I can do nothing, but praise God, I'm _____ (Heb. 13:5)!
   A. Doing the best I can
   B. Not without the Word
   C. Not without the Law
   D. All of the above
   E. None of the above
   E. None of the above

5. Toward the end of their forty years in the wilderness, the Israelites were without water for a second time (Ex. 17:6). This time, the Lord told Moses to speak to the rock instead of striking it (Num. 20:8), but Moses struck the rock twice instead. The Lord told Moses that he would not live to enter into the Promised Land because of his disobedience in striking the rock (Num. 20:10-12). I believe the real issue here was Moses' self-will. God told him to speak to the rock, but Moses thought it would be more dramatic to hit it. He was exerting his own wisdom and trying to do things his own way again. If God had failed to deal with Moses' self-will, the entire nation of Israel could have spent another forty years in the wilderness—God did this to protect Israel from Moses. We don't ever learn the lesson of humility completely: It's not like we have one encounter with the Lord and then never again have to deal with leaning on our own understanding or ability. Some people think everything in the Christian life is supposed to work perfectly after they believe, but it doesn't happen that way. *God uses us in spite of who we are, not because of who we are.* We need to lay our lives down before God—give Him control. God will take our offering and give us back His life and power in return.

5a. Why didn't Moses live to enter into the Promised Land?
Because of his disobedience in striking the rock (i.e., his self-will)

5b. Discussion question: Do you agree with the statement "We don't ever learn the lesson of humility completely"? Why or why not?
Discussion question

5c. God uses you in spite of who you are, not _____ of who you are.
Because

8. What do you need to recognize?

_____

_____

_____

9. Discussion question: What does it mean to make a total surrender to God and yield to Him?

_____

_____

_____

10. True or false: The Lord told Moses that He would take care of everything and that Moses didn't have to do anything.

11. Discussion question: In what ways can you live out the ideas that your life is not your own, Christ lives through you, and you need to use the power He has given you to improve your situation (Gal. 2:20)?

_____

_____

_____

12. Without Christ, I can do nothing, but praise God, I'm _____ (Heb. 13:5)!
    A. Doing the best I can
    B. Not without the Word
    C. Not without the Law
    D. All of the above
    E. None of the above

13. Why didn't Moses live to enter into the Promised Land?

_____

_____

_____

14. Discussion question: Do you agree with the statement "We don't ever learn the lesson of humility completely"? Why or why not?

_____

_____

_____

15. God uses you in spite of who you are, not _____ of who you are.

8. That you cannot accomplish God's will in your own strength
9. *Discussion question*
10. False
11. *Discussion question*
12. E.   None of the above
13. Because of his disobedience in striking the rock (i.e., his self-will)
14. *Discussion question*
15. Because

EXODUS 14:12-16

Is not this the word that we did tell thee in Egypt, saying, Let us alone, that we may serve the Egyptians? For it had been better for us to serve the Egyptians, than that we should die in the wilderness. [13] And Moses said unto the people, Fear ye not, stand still, and see the salvation of the LORD, which he will shew to you to day: for the Egyptians whom ye have seen to day, ye shall see them again no more for ever. [14] The LORD shall fight for you, and ye shall hold your peace. [15] And the LORD said unto Moses, Wherefore criest thou unto me? speak unto the children of Israel, that they go forward: [16] But lift thou up thy rod, and stretch out thine hand over the sea, and divide it: and the children of Israel shall go on dry ground through the midst of the sea.

GALATIANS 2:20

I am crucified with Christ: nevertheless I live; yet not I, but Christ liveth in me: and the life which I now live in the flesh I live by the faith of the Son of God, who loved me, and gave himself for me.

JAMES 4:7

Submit yourselves therefore to God. Resist the devil, and he will flee from you.

PHILIPPIANS 4:13

I can do all things through Christ which strengtheneth me.

HEBREWS 13:5

Let your conversation be without covetousness; and be content with such things as ye have: for he hath said, I will never leave thee, nor forsake thee.

EXODUS 17:6

Behold, I will stand before thee there upon the rock in Horeb; and thou shalt smite the rock, and there shall come water out of it, that the people may drink. And Moses did so in the sight of the elders of Israel.

NUMBERS 20:8

Take the rod, and gather thou the assembly together, thou, and Aaron thy brother, and speak ye unto the rock before their eyes; and it shall give forth his water, and thou shalt bring forth to them water out of the rock: so thou shalt give the congregation and their beasts drink.

NUMBERS 20:10-12

And Moses and Aaron gathered the congregation together before the rock, and he said unto them, Hear now, ye rebels; must we fetch you water out of this rock? [11] And Moses lifted up his hand, and with his rod he smote the rock twice: and the water came out abundantly, and the congregation drank, and their beasts also. [12] And the LORD spake unto Moses and Aaron, Because ye believed me not, to sanctify me in the eyes of the children of Israel, therefore ye shall not bring this congregation into the land which I have given them.

1 CORINTHIANS 10:4

And did all drink the same spiritual drink: for they drank of that spiritual Rock that followed them: and that Rock was Christ.

HEBREWS 6:6

If they shall fall away, to renew them again unto repentance; seeing they crucify to themselves the Son of God afresh, and put him to an open shame.

LET PEACE
RULE

LESSON 9

And let the peace of God rule in your hearts, to the which also ye are called in one body; and be ye thankful.

COLOSSIANS 3:15

The Greek word for *"rule"* comes from the root word from which we get our English word "umpire," which means "to govern or arbitrate." We can understand this in the same way we understand the function of an umpire in baseball: Once the umpire makes the call—it is decided. The pitcher hurls the ball toward home plate, and the umpire calls it either a ball or a strike. His decision is final; there's no debate, no chance for a redo. The peace of God should act just like an umpire in our hearts—deciding which opportunities we should act on and which ones we should let pass by.

Peace is a fruit of the Holy Spirit, so you always have peace in your born-again spirit (Gal. 5:22-23). You may not always feel peace, because you aren't always living out of your spirit. You can get caught up in your emotions or your thinking, but peace is always present within you. All you have to do is shut off the things that dominate you from the outside and follow the peace that is in your spirit.

The Holy Spirit is constantly bearing witness in our hearts, but not always with words. Sometimes we just feel peace, or a lack of it, about doing something. We shouldn't do anything unless we have peace in our hearts about doing it. This principle is the flip side of delighting ourselves in the Lord (Ps. 37:4).

Many years ago, I planned a trip to Costa Rica. I had ministered there before and had a tremendous response, so they invited me back. I purchased my plane tickets early and was looking forward to preaching there again. A few weeks before the trip, I helped my mother move. While driving the moving truck from Texas to Colorado, I began to pray about my ministry opportunity in Costa Rica. As I prayed about the trip, I lost all desire to go. On the previous trip, we saw some terrific things happen and had a great time, so there wasn't any reason for me not to want to go back. I just lost my desire to go.

I knew I needed to make sure I was hearing from God and not merely feeling an emotional reaction, so during the seventeen-hour drive to Colorado, I worshiped God and prayed in tongues. The more I focused on God, the less I wanted to go to Costa Rica. I decided to let the peace of God rule in my heart. I couldn't come up with any particular reason, but I had zero peace about going. So, I canceled my meeting, and the people hosting the meeting got really upset. They had already done a lot of advertising and wanted to know why I was canceling. I told them I didn't have a reason, that I just didn't want to go. Of course, that wasn't a very spiritual answer, so they were offended. I didn't know what to say to them except that I had lost my peace about going.

Three weeks later, I was at home in Colorado when I heard about a flight out of Mexico City that crashed during take-off. Everyone onboard the plane died. I think that's why the Lord took away my peace for that trip. If I had gone ahead with the meeting simply because I didn't have a logical reason to call it off, I probably would have died in that plane crash. But instead, I let the peace of God act as an umpire—and it saved my life!

Before this happened, I had learned the hard way to trust the leading of God's peace in my heart. While pastoring a church in Pritchett, Colorado, we saw a man raised from the dead, witnessed great things, and were making a difference in the community. Our church grew to 100 members in a town of only 144 people!

The few people who were in leadership in the church before I came were custom combiners. They were gone for six months out of the year harvesting crops. They wanted to put a new elder in place to help me run the church while they were gone, so they suggested a man who had been the only person to embrace me when I first arrived in town. He was a neat guy who was excited about what we were teaching. I didn't have any reason not to want him as an elder, except I didn't feel peace about it in my heart.

I told the other leaders I didn't feel good about having him as an elder. They said, "Why not? Tell us what's wrong with him?" But I didn't have an answer. I didn't know of anything that was wrong with him. They countered by telling me all of the reasons he looked like a good choice, yet all I had to say was, "I don't feel good about it." We talked for a long time, and they basically shamed me until I gave in. By the end of the meeting, it was agreed that he would become the new elder.

Within a week after the combiners left town to go harvest wheat, the new elder turned into the devil personified. He started rumors that I was drinking, committing adultery, doing drugs, and stealing money from the church. Even though I didn't even take a salary from the church, he accused me of *anything* and *everything* you could think of. I had nothing but problems from him. It was *terrible.*

When all of this happened, I thought, *I knew in my heart that we shouldn't have made him an elder!* I didn't feel peace about it and went with logic instead of what I felt in my heart. I decided right then that I would never make the same mistake again. Since then, to the best of my ability, I have always let the peace of God rule in my heart.

A year or two after this incident, I felt a lack of peace about going to Costa Rica. Since I had learned my lesson about the elder and not following my peace, I wasn't about to ignore the lack of peace I was feeling in this situation—and it probably saved my life!

I think nearly everyone has encountered a similar experience some time in their lives. At some time or another, we have all been at a major crossroad and made a logical decision that went against what we felt led to do in our hearts. We wanted to go one way, but all logic and counsel suggested that we go in another—so we went with the logical decision. As soon as everything fell apart, we said, "I knew I wasn't supposed to do that." For no particular reason, we *knew* we weren't supposed to do it, but we did it anyway because it looked like the right thing to do. When we listen, we will hear God speaking to us and leading us in the right direction.

Big and Little

Letting the peace of God rule in our hearts is one of the best ways to discern His leadership. He will put a desire in our hearts, then it's up to us to evaluate whether or not we feel peace about doing it—to confirm that it's from Him. We need to spend extra time seeking the Lord to see if the idea still excites and blesses us. This not only applies to big decisions, like our life-long vocations; it applies to life's little details as well. Does God want you to hire a particular employee or buy a certain house? It's pretty simple. I pray about things, and whatever I have the most peace about doing is what I go with.

We bought the building that our ministry is currently in for 3.25 million dollars, which was a huge step for us. We had to take out a loan to get the building. It was just an empty warehouse that needed another 3.2 million dollars worth of renovations. After we purchased the building, we spent nine months trying to obtain a construction loan for the renovations.

Initially, the lender guaranteed us the construction loan. They said, "We wouldn't give you a loan for the building if we weren't planning to give you the construction loan." For nine months, the banker kept telling us that we would get the loan "next week." It was a difficult situation and we needed to do something, but they wouldn't give us the money. Finally, the banker said, "Why don't we just start the whole process over? We'll get a new appraisal and start the whole process over."

All I could see was another nine months of delays. Something didn't seem right, so I started praying. As I was praying that afternoon, I remembered some things the Lord had spoken to me two years earlier. Someone had given me a prophecy that I wouldn't need to take out a loan, because I already had my *own* bank. When the Holy Spirit brought that to my remembrance, I thought, *I have my own bank? Where is it?* Then I recalled the rest of the prophecy: My ministry partners would be my financing. Somehow or another, I hadn't associated the prophecy with the building program. As I was praying, the Lord brought the prophecy back to me and said, "I don't want you to take out a loan. I'm going to pay for this."

I don't know if you can relate to coming up with 3.2 million dollars, but at the rate our ministry was saving, it would have taken us more than a hundred years to come up with that kind of money! Obviously, that wasn't going to work. I knew that a commitment to renovate the building, without taking out a loan would kill the ministry unless God came through in a big way. But I felt that God was leading me to trust Him for the money, so I wouldn't go back on the decision once it was made. Scripture says that a godly man will swear to his own hurt and change not (Ps. 15:4), so I told people that if I was going to do it debt free, then I would do it debt free even if it took me a hundred years!

It was a big decision. Once I had the desire in my heart to build debt free, I prayed about it for a week or two and then let the peace of God rule in my heart. The decision was potentially disastrous for the future of our ministry. We didn't have any evidence to suggest that we could raise 3.2 million dollars, but I had peace about it—so we decided to start the renovations without taking out a loan. Fourteen months later, we had 3.2 million dollars, the building was finished, and we moved in without the debt of a construction loan. It was one of the best decisions I have ever made. Even though it was illogical, we did it because I had peace in my heart about it. God's supernatural provision came through for us.

Peace, Be Still

Be still, and know that I am God.

PSALM 46:10

I believe we have made the Christian life harder than it needs to be. It's not difficult to have God lead us. We just love God with our whole hearts and commit our lives unto Him—then as we delight in the Lord, He will put His desires in our hearts. When we come to a fork in the road, we just need to go in the direction we have the most peace about. But we can't live this way if we are constantly flooding our minds with the noise and junk of this world. Most Christians do not seek God or spend enough time in His presence to really feel what is in their hearts. They are led by external things, being pushed along in life by the crowd. Sometimes we have to be still in order to hear our hearts.

Once I had a dream in which I saw a big banner with "Psalm 46:10" written on it. I have quoted this verse a thousand times, but at that moment, I couldn't remember that verse to save my life. So, I got out of bed, opened up my Bible, and found the scripture. It was such a vivid dream that I sat there thinking about that verse. I didn't know exactly what "being still" meant, but I decided that I was going to try being physically still, just to see if that was part of it.

Later that day, Jamie went shopping, so I was at the house alone for a while. I went outside, sat down in a chair, and for an hour and a half, I never moved anything but my eyes. I sat as still as I possibly could. I wanted to see what would happen if I was really still. It took me a while to get totally still, but after I did, I started noticing things that I normally wouldn't have noticed.

We live in the Colorado mountains—where there's a lot of wildlife. I saw thousands of ants I had never noticed before. A deer walked so close to me that I could almost touch it. I became so still that even a chipmunk came and sat on my foot. Sounds, like the wind blowing through the trees, that I never really paid any attention to, became loud. I became aware of all of these things that I typically never noticed before, because I was always too busy going somewhere or doing something.

This principle can be applied to us spiritually as well. Sometimes we have to be still—no television or radio noise in the background. Instead of always talking when we pray, sometimes we need to be still and listen. I have a friend who spouts words like a machine gun when he prays. Once he gets going, he doesn't stop—*then he wonders why God never speaks to him.* God can't get a word in edge-wise. We need to pretend like we are praying through a two-way radio every once in a while and say "Over," to give God a chance to speak. When we are still, the things that are in our hearts come out and we begin to hear God speak to us.

This is one reason that people who aren't seeking the Lord hate to be still. When we are still, a little homing device God has planted in all of us starts going off. It makes us think about our lives and question whether or not we are experiencing all there is. People who are not seeking God don't want to be confronted by Him, so they drown Him out. They always have the television or music on—they are always doing something. They can't be still, because their thoughts will lead them to God, and they don't want to go there.

Life can get to be a treadmill that keeps you from resting because you are too busy just trying to keep up the pace. When you are on the treadmill, you don't have time to ask yourself, "Is this the life I want? Is this what God wants for me?" Many people go years without sitting down to take an inventory of their lives.

Everyone needs to look at their lives now and again to inspect their options. See what your desires are, and seek God to find out what you have peace about doing. Ask yourself where you want to be in five, ten, or twenty years. Are you doing what you want to be doing? Is your life headed in the direction you want it to be going? If you don't have peace about where you are right now or where you are going, you need to start making some changes.

If you aren't absolutely sure what changes to make, just start testing the waters. A boat has to be moving for the rudder to steer it. The rudder won't do anything when the boat is sitting still. In the same way, you have to be moving before God can give you direction. If you aren't sure what God wants you to do, let the peace of God rule in your heart and start taking small steps in the direction you have peace about. As you begin to step out, God can guide you. All of a sudden, things will begin to fall in line and you will see God moving in your life—which will encourage you to go a little further.

When I first started seeking God, I did all kinds of things. You might have to try a number of avenues before you find the right one. You might start off in one direction, only to see everything go wrong and lose all of your peace. Sometimes the way you discern God's will is by finding out what He *doesn't* want you to do—like when He gives you a *holy dissatisfaction*. If you don't have peace about what you are doing then don't go that direction.

I know this isn't deep—it's practical—and it can change your life. Anybody can do what I'm talking about. Every time you face a decision, God is speaking to you and giving you direction. He may not speak in an audible voice, but He will guide you. Often, God will guide you by the peace in your heart. I believe that most people who seek God's will for their lives would discover significant direction simply by being still and allowing God's peace to rule in their hearts. Jesus is the Prince of Peace, and He will show you the way you need to go.

OUTLINE • 9

I. The Greek word for *"rule"* in Colossians 3:15 comes from our English word "umpire," which means "to govern or arbitrate."

   A. We can understand this in the same way we understand the function of an umpire in baseball: Once the umpire makes the call, his decision is final; there's no debate.

   B. The peace of God should act just like an umpire in our hearts.

   C. Peace is a fruit of the Holy Spirit, so we always have peace in our born-again spirits.

   D. The Holy Spirit is constantly bearing witness in our hearts, but not always with words.

   E. Sometimes we just feel peace, or a lack of it, about doing something.

II. God will put a desire in our hearts, then it's up to us to evaluate whether or not we feel peace about doing it—to confirm what is from God.

   Be still, and know that I am God: I will be exalted among the heathen, I will be exalted in the earth.
   PSALM 46:10

   A. When we come to a fork in the toad, we need to go in the direction we have the most peace.

   B. Instead of always talking when we pray, sometimes we need to be still and listen.

   C. People who aren't seeking the Lord hate to be still.

   D. When we are still, a little homing device God has planted in all of us starts going off, making us think about our lives and question whether or not we are experiencing all there is.

   E. If we don't have peace about where we are right now or where we are going, we need to start making some changes—we need to start taking small steps in the direction we have peace about.

   F. Sometimes the way we discern God's will is by finding out what He *doesn't* want us to do—like when He gives us a *holy dissatisfaction*.

   G. This is practical and can change our lives.

   H. I believe that most people who seek God's will for their lives would discover significant direction simply by being still and allowing God's peace to rule in their hearts.

1. The Greek word for *"rule"* in Colossians 3:15 comes from our English word "umpire," which means "to govern or arbitrate." We can understand this in the same way we understand the function of an umpire in baseball: Once the umpire makes the call, his decision is final; there's no debate. The peace of God should act just like an umpire in our hearts. Peace is a fruit of the Holy Spirit, so we always have peace in our born-again spirits. The Holy Spirit is constantly bearing witness in our hearts, but not always with words. Sometimes we just feel peace, or a lack of it, about doing something.

1a. The peace of God should rule like an _____ in your heart.
Umpire

1b. True or false: Regarding peace, God won't always use words to bear witness in your heart.
True

1c. Discussion question: Have you ever experienced peace, or a lack of it, about doing something? Explain.
Discussion question

2. God will put a desire in our hearts, then it's up to us to evaluate whether or not we feel peace about doing it—to confirm what is from God.

> *Be still, and know that I am God: I will be exalted among the heathen, I will be exalted in the earth.*
>
> PSALM 46:10

When we come to a fork in the toad, we need to go in the direction we have the most peace. People who aren't seeking the Lord hate to be still. Instead of always talking when we pray, sometimes we need to be still and listen. When we are still, a little homing device God has planted in all of us starts going off, making us think about our lives and question whether or not we are experiencing all there is. If we don't have peace about where we are right now or where we are going, we need to start making some changes—we need to start taking small steps in the direction we have peace about. Sometimes the way we discern God's will is by finding out what He *doesn't* want us to do—like when He gives us a *holy dissatisfaction*. This is practical and can change our lives. I believe that most people who seek God's will for their lives would discover significant direction simply by being still and allowing God's peace to rule in their hearts.

2a. When God puts a desire in your heart, what do you have to do?

    A. Evaluate whether or not you feel peace about doing it—to confirm what is from God
    B. First make sure everyone who is important to you in your life agrees with it
    C. Check it against your to-do list, and trash it if it's not on there
    D. Sleep on it
    E. Ask God to give you a sign
    A. Evaluate whether or not you feel peace about doing it—to confirm what is from God

2b. Instead of always talking when you pray, you need to be _____ and listen.
    Still

2c. Sometimes the way you discern God's will is by finding out what He _____ want you to do.
    Doesn't

2d. What is that like?
    A holy dissatisfaction

2e. Discussion question: What does it take for you to be still and let God's peace rule in\ your heart?
    Discussion question

DISCIPLESHIP QUESTIONS • 9

1. The peace of God should rule like an _____ in your heart.

2. True or false: Regarding peace, God won't always use words to bear witness in your heart.

3. Discussion question: Have you ever experienced peace, or a lack of it, about doing something? Explain.

   _____

   _____

   _____

4. When God puts a desire in your heart, what do you have to do?
   A. Evaluate whether or not you feel peace about doing it—to confirm what is from God
   B. First make sure everyone who is important to you in your life agrees with it
   C. Check it against your to-do list, and trash it if it's not on there
   D. Sleep on it
   E. Ask God to give you a sign

5. Instead of always talking when you pray, you need to be _____ and listen.

6. Sometimes the way you discern God's will is by finding out what He _____ want you to do.

7. What is that like?

   _____

   _____

   _____

8. Discussion question: What does it take for you to be still and let God's peace rule in your heart?

   _____

   _____

   _____

ANSWER KEY • 9

1. Umpire
2. True
3. *Discussion question*
4. A. Evaluate whether or not you feel peace about doing it—to confirm what is from God
5. Still
6. Doesn't
7. A holy dissatisfaction
8. *Discussion question*

COLOSSIANS 3:15

And let the peace of God rule in your hearts, to which also ye are called in one body; and be ye thankful.

GALATIANS 3:22-23

But the fruit of the Spirit is love, joy, peace, longsuffering, gentleness, goodness, faith, [23] Meekness, temperance: against such there is no law.

PSALM 37:4

Delight thyself also in the Lord; and he shall give thee the desires of thine heart.

PSALM 15:4

In whose eyes a vile person is contemned; but he honoureth them that fear the Lord. He that sweareth to his own hurt, and changeth not.

PSALM 46:10

Be still, and know that I am God: I will be exalted among the heathen, I will be exalted in the earth.

THE HOLY
SPIRIT

LESSON 10.1

But as it is written, Eye hath not seen, nor ear heard, neither have entered into the heart of man, the things which God hath prepared for them that love him.

1 CORINTHIANS 2:9

The Apostle Paul was in the middle of defending his authority to the Corinthians when he wrote this scripture. He was quoting an Old Testament verse, but a large portion of the church has used this scripture to embrace the idea that we can never understand God or expect victory in this life. God's ways *are* higher than our ways (Is. 55:8-9)—but that doesn't mean He can't reveal Himself to us or lead us into victory. Paul was merely saying that in our natural physical ability—apart from the inspiration and the revelation of the Holy Spirit—we can't understand God. People stop at this verse and say, "See, we can't know God." But we shouldn't stop there; we have to keep reading:

But God hath revealed them unto us by his Spirit: for the Spirit searcheth all things, yea, the deep things of God. [11] For what man knoweth the things of a man, save the spirit of man which is in him? even so the things of God knoweth no man, but the Spirit of God. [12] Now we have received, not the spirit of the world, but the spirit which is of God; that we might know the things that are freely given to us of God.

1 CORINTHIANS 2:10-12

Paul wasn't saying we can't *know*; he was saying that in ourselves, without the inspiration of God, we can't know His will. In our natural minds, we don't know everything, but we have a mind in our spirits. These scriptures say that our born-again spirits have been infused with the knowledge of God—so we *can* understand the things of God.

Our spirits know everything we need to know. We already have wisdom in our spirits. God understands that we live in a physical world, and the Scripture says that if any man lacks wisdom, let him ask God (James 1:5). The wisdom we receive doesn't come from heaven.

God has already abounded toward us in all wisdom and prudence (Eph. 1:8). The Bible says we have a special anointing, or power, from God and our spirits know all things (1 John 2:20). *Our job is to draw out what God has already put in us.*

Unless we know how to draw out the wisdom and power of God from our spirits, we will end up trying to discern God's will by judging our circumstances. King David wrote that no one should be like a horse or mule, which have no understanding and must be led around by bit and bridle (Ps. 32:8-9). We are supposed to be led by God, not our circumstances. Isaiah prophesied that we would hear a voice behind us saying, "This is the way, walk thou in it" (Is. 30:21). We should be led by the still, small voice of God (1 Kin. 19:12-13). Allowing our circumstances to dictate our course of action is no different from a mule being pulled this way and that way by a bit.

One night, the Apostle Paul had a dream of a man from Macedonia calling him over to help them (Acts 16:9). When he woke up in the morning, he knew that dream meant God was sending him to minister to the people of Macedonia. So, Paul and Silas traveled to Macedonia and entered the city of Philippi. Within days they, were arrested, beaten, and locked in the lowest part of the dungeon (Acts 16:22-24).

In similar circumstances, I think most of us would have say, "Well, this must not have been God." We would reason that God would never lead us to do something that would land us in jail. But circumstances are not a reliable indicator of God's will. Paul *was* following God's leading, and going to Philippi was *exactly* what God told him to do. Letting circumstances dictate is not an accurate way to discern God's will.

The spirit on the inside of us knows all things (1 John 2:20 with Col. 3:10 and 1 Cor. 2:16). Part of following God's will involves learning to listen to the voice of God inside of us and obeying it no matter what. In our spirits, we have supernatural God-ordained wisdom; by tapping into it, we will begin to see things that are hidden to our natural minds.

Drawing It Out

Howbeit we speak wisdom among them that are perfect: yet not the wisdom of this world, nor of the princes of this world, that come to nought: [7] But we speak the wisdom of God in a mystery, even the hidden wisdom, which God ordained before the world unto our glory.

1 CORINTHIANS 2:6-7

God's wisdom trumps natural wisdom. Paul said, *"We speak the wisdom of God in a mystery, even the hidden wisdom."* Wisdom that is hidden from the natural mind, but it isn't hidden *from* you—it is hidden *for* you.

One of the first things I did when the news media announced that the economy was in recession was to start boldly proclaiming that God supplies all of my needs according to His riches in glory by Christ Jesus (Phil. 4:19). I'm not limited to this world's economy and God has proven it. In the first six months after the recession hit in October 2008, the stock that Jamie and I owned made a 61 percent profit—while the stock market itself went down 51%. You can do the same thing if you believe that God is your source, instead of this natural world.

Every month since October 2008, our ministry's income has exceeded income for that same month in previous years. I think our increase was something like 28 percent this past year—during a "recession." The wisdom of the world would tell you it's not possible to prosper during an economic downturn in the way we have, but our prosperity isn't coming by using the wisdom of this world.

This is another example of why renewing our minds with the Word of God is essential. God's Word reveals His will, and knowing His will gives us the faith to believe for the impossible—and see it come to pass. Knowledge of God's Word is power. It's how we know what God has promised us and what we can have faith to believe He will supply. But aside from reading the Word, the Apostle Paul reveals another way for us to tap into the wisdom in our spirits:

> *Follow after charity, and desire spiritual gifts, but rather that ye may prophesy.*
> *[2] For he that speaketh in an unknown tongue speaketh not unto men, but unto God: for no man understandeth him; howbeit in the spirit he speaketh mysteries.*
> 1 CORINTHIANS 14:1-2

This scripture is part of the same letter in which the Apostle Paul said, *"We speak the wisdom of God in a mystery."* (1 Cor. 2:6-7) In this verse, he says that when you are speaking in tongues, you are speaking mysteries. Paul was a man who helped change the world. It was said of him that he was among those who *"turned the world upside down"* (Acts 17:6). He wrote almost half of the New Testament. Do you know where he received all that wisdom from?

When he was born again, God put His supernatural wisdom in Paul's born-again spirit. Just as any other believer, Paul had an unction from the Holy One and he knew all things (1 John 2:20)—he had the mind of Christ (1 Cor. 2:16). Paul says he drew the knowledge out of his spirit by speaking in tongues. Even though our spirits know all things, we still have to get the knowledge into our natural understanding. Paul said,

> *For if I pray in an unknown tongue, my spirit prayeth, but my understanding is unfruitful.*
> 1 CORINTHIANS 14:14

When we speak in tongues, our spirits pray—the part of us that knows all things (1 John 2:20), is renewed in knowledge (Col. 3:10), and has the mind of Christ (1 Cor. 2:16). This is the same part of us that always has peace and love; it doesn't have any questions or problems. Our spirits pray the hidden wisdom of God in a mystery, under the inspiration of the Holy Spirit.

One of the most important things we can do when we come up against a difficult situation is pray in tongues. Our born-again spirits, which have the mind of Christ and know all things, pray our answer when we speak in tongues. Our spirits pray the wisdom we need and give us instruction. Scripture says that when we speak in tongues, our understanding is unfruitful. In other words, our minds don't understand what we are saying. But Paul tells us how to unravel the mystery:

> *Wherefore let him that speaketh in an unknown tongue pray that he may interpret.*
> 1 CORINTHIANS 14:13

We are speaking the hidden wisdom of God when we pray in tongues. It isn't gibberish; it's just that our minds don't understand spiritual things. As we pray, the wisdom of God comes right out of our mouths. It comes out in a language we don't understand; we just need to get an interpretation. Speaking in tongues is like flipping a supernatural switch—we turn on a powerful generator and the life and wisdom of God that are in our spirits start coming out of our mouths. All we have to do is ask God to give us an interpretation of what we are praying from our spirits, and He will reveal to us the wisdom we are speaking in tongues.

In a church service, Paul gave instruction that if anyone spoke in tongues, it must be interpreted in a language that the people understand so all of the listeners will be edified (1 Cor. 14:27-28). But speaking in tongues isn't just for church services. Paul said,

> *I thank my God, I speak with tongues more than ye all: Yet in the church I had rather speak five words with my understanding, that by my voice I might teach others also, than ten thousand words in an unknown tongue"*
> 1 CORINTHIANS 14:18-19

He spoke in tongues more than the entire church of Corinth put together. He didn't do most of this during church; he spoke in tongues privately.

Speaking in tongues isn't just for the purpose of prophecy or ministering to other people. The gift of tongues that operates in a church service is a ministry of the Holy Spirit, given to edify and build up the church body—not everybody has that gift. That gift of tongues is what Scripture is talking about when it says, *"Do all speak with tongues?"* The obvious answer is no (1 Cor 12:30), but that statement is a reference to the *gift* of speaking in tongues and interpretation that function within a church service. Not everybody has a *ministry* of speaking in tongues, but every born-again believer who is filled with the Holy Spirit has *the ability* to speak in tongues. Jesus said, *"and these signs shall follow them that believe; In my name shall they cast out devils; they shall speak with new tongues"* (Mark 16:17).

Edify Yourself

Speaking in tongues is not something you do one time in church in order to prove that you are filled with the Holy Spirit; it's something you should be doing on a regular basis. It's your spirit man praying. Your spirit is where your new life is—it's where the power of God is. Your natural mind doesn't understand what your spirit is praying, but that is to be expected.

> *But the natural man receiveth not the things of the Spirit of God: for they are foolishness unto him: neither can he know them, because they are spiritually discerned.*
>
> 1 CORINTHIANS 2:14

Spiritual things are foolishness to the natural mind. If you speak in tongues for more than five minutes, your mind is going to say, *This is silly. What am I doing?* The carnal part of you will rise up and try to get you back into the natural realm, where it feels comfortable. You have to make a decision to continue speaking in tongues in spite of what your mind is thinking. You edify yourself when you speak in tongues (1 Cor. 14:4) and promote spiritual growth. Speaking in tongues is an act of faith; it requires you to cross the barrier between carnal thinking and being focused on God.

It is impossible for you to pray in tongues over a long period of time and keep your mind focused on carnal, ungodly things. A mind that is focused on carnal things is not attentive to spiritual things, because the carnal mind is hostile to God. So, a mind focused on the information coming in through your five senses will always be opposed to God. On the other hand, if you persist in speaking in tongues, your attention will shift to spiritual things— which bring life and peace (Rom. 8:6-7).

You can do something with your mind as you pray in tongues and still have perfect comprehension, because your spirit is praying—not your brain. You can read the Bible while you are speaking in tongues and understand what you are reading perfectly. You can't do that quoting *Mary Had a Little Lamb*, because you are quoting out of your mind and trying to read with your mind at the same time. But when you are praying in tongues, your spirit is praying—not your brain. This is one of the things that reveals that speaking in tongues is supernatural. You aren't just making up words. The sounds don't come from your brain; they come out of your spirit.

When I first started speaking in tongues, I used to do it for one to five hours a day. I discovered that while the spirit is praying, the brain is unoccupied. You can't turn your brain off, so it's going to think about something. The mind will wander while you are praying in tongues and start thinking of all sorts of things. The way I dealt with this was to pray with my mind as I prayed with my spirit. This helped me focus my thoughts on God.

As I prayed, things would suddenly come to me. I would think of people I hadn't thought of in years. All of a sudden, they would come to mind, so I would pray for them with my mind—at the same time I was praying in tongues out of my mouth. At first, I didn't connect the two, but when I was done praying, I would call the person that came to my mind and talk to them. Each time, it was an answer to prayer and they would say, "You must have been hearing from God to call me right now."

One time, God put a friend of mine on my heart as I was praying in tongues, so I felt like calling him. His wife answered the phone when I called, and as soon as she heard my voice, she hung up. I thought to myself, *Boy, that went really well.* As I was sitting there trying to figure out what I might have done wrong, she called back a moment later and explained what was going on. Her husband had just been forced out of the ministry because of some bad decisions. They lost their home, and she was living with her mother at nearly sixty years old. Their entire life had come undone.

She said, "We've traveled the world helping other people, and I was just sitting here praying 'God, why don't you have somebody minster to us? I know we are living with my mother and our phone number has changed, but you're God—you could at least have somebody call. If You really love us, why don't you have somebody call?'"

The phone rang right when she finished praying. She picked it up and heard me say, "This is Andrew Wommack." She was so shocked that she hung up. But then she called back and I was able to minister to her. *When you pray in tongues, God will speak to you and reveal things that you can't know with your physical mind.*

On another occasion, Jamie and I felt led to stop in a little town of 100 people while we were driving through the middle of *nowhere* in Colorado. We stopped to see some old friends we hadn't spoken to for over a decade. They thought we were a little too radical and had tried to turn us away from the ministry, creating a rift between us. The town was small, so it was pretty easy to find out where the Baptist pastor lived.

We knocked on the front door, and my old friend Joseph opened it. The moment he saw me, all of the blood drained out of his face. He stood there looking at me and didn't say a word. So, I asked if we could come inside, and he silently turned aside to let us walk in. We walked in, and his wife was kneeling down praying at the coffee table. She looked up and turned white also.

We all sat down, but they just stared at us white-faced and silent. Finally, I asked, "Is everything okay?" Joseph told me they had resigned their position at the church and their life was in turmoil. He said they had just been kneeling around the coffee table asking God to send someone to help them. They said, "We'll take anybody, Lord…*anybody*." Our knock at the door came while they were still praying. We were the last people they would normally have let in, but God put us together supernaturally, and we became great friends again. God also restored them and put them back in the ministry. It was awesome!

OUTLINE • 10.1

I. Based on 1 Corinthians 2:9, a large portion of the church has embraced the idea that we can never understand God or expect victory in this life.

   A. But we shouldn't stop at this verse; we should keep reading:

But God hath revealed them unto us by his Spirit: for the Spirit searcheth all things, yea, the deep things of God. [11] For what man knoweth the things of a man, save the spirit of man which is in him? even so the things of God knoweth no man, but the Spirit of God. [12] Now we have received, not the spirit of the world, but the spirit which is of God; that we might know the things that are freely given to us of God.

1 CORINTHIANS 2:10-12

   B. Paul was saying that in ourselves, without the inspiration of God, we can't know His will.

   C. These scriptures say that our born-again spirits have been infused with the knowledge of God—so we *can* understand the things of God.

   D. The Bible says we have a special anointing, or power, from God and our spirits know all things (1 John 2:20).

   E. Unless we know how to draw out the ways of God from our spirits, we will end up trying to discern God's will by judging circumstances.

II. Paul said, *"We speak the wisdom of God in a mystery, even the hidden wisdom of God"* (1 Cor. 2:7).

   A. Paul says he drew the knowledge out of his spirit by speaking in tongues.

For if I pray in an unknown tongue, my spirit prayeth, but my understanding is unfruitful.

1 CORINTHIANS 14:14

   B. When we speak in tongues, our spirits pray—the part of us that knows all things (1 John 2:20), is renewed in knowledge (Col. 3:10), and has the mind of Christ (1 Cor. 2:16).

   C. Our minds don't understand what we are saying, but Paul tells us how to unravel the mystery:

Wherefore let him that speaketh in an unknown tongue pray that he may interpret.

1 CORINTHIANS 14:13

   D. All we have to do is ask God to give us an interpretation of what we are praying from our spirits, and He will reveal to us the wisdom we are speaking in tongues.

   E. Speaking in tongues isn't just for the purpose of prophecy or ministering to other people.

III. Every born-again believer who is filled with the Holy Spirit has *the ability* to speak in tongues.

> *And these signs shall follow them that believe; In my name shall they cast out devils; they shall speak with new tongues.*
>
> MARK 16:17

A. It's not something you do one time in church in order to prove that you are filled with the Holy Spirit; it's something you should be doing on a regular basis.

B. You edify yourself when you speak in tongues (1 Cor. 14:4) and promote spiritual growth.

C. Speaking in tongues is an act of faith; it requires you to cross the barrier between carnal thinking and being focused on God—it is impossible for you to pray in tongues over a long period of time and keep your mind focused on carnal, ungodly things.

D. If you persist in speaking in tongues, your attention will shift to spiritual things—which bring life and peace (Rom. 8:6-7).

IV. You can do something with your mind as you pray in tongues and still have perfect comprehension.

A. The mind will wander while you are praying in tongues and start thinking of all sorts of things.

B. What helped me to focus my thoughts on God was to pray with my mind as I prayed with my spirit.

C. As I prayed, things would suddenly come to me.

   i. I would think of people I hadn't thought of in years.

   ii. So, I would pray for them with my mind—at the same time I was praying in tongues out of my mouth.

   iii. I would call the person and talk to them, and each time, it was an answer to prayer.

D. *When you pray in tongues, God will speak to you and reveal things that you can't know with your physical mind.*

TEACHER'S GUIDE • 10.1

1. Based on 1 Corinthians 2:9, a large portion of the church has embraced the idea that we can never understand God or expect victory in this life. But we shouldn't stop at this verse; we should keep reading:

> But God hath revealed them unto us by his Spirit: for the Spirit searcheth all things, yea, the deep things of God. *[11]* For what man knoweth the things of a man, save the spirit of man which is in him? even so the things of God knoweth no man, but the Spirit of God. *[12]* Now we have received, not the spirit of the world, but the spirit which is of God; that we might know the things that are freely given to us of God.
>
> 1 CORINTHIANS 2:10-12

Paul was saying that in ourselves, without the inspiration of God, we can't know His will. These scriptures say that our born-again spirits have been infused with the knowledge of God—so we *can* understand the things of God. The Bible says we have a special anointing, or power, from God and our spirits know all things (1 John 2:20). Unless we know how to draw out the ways of God from our spirits, we will end up trying to discern God's will by judging circumstances.

1a. Discussion question: Why is it important to not build a doctrine around one verse but to keep reading?
Discussion question

1b. You can _____ the things of God.
Understand

1c. Discussion question: How would you apply 1 John 2:20 to your life?
Discussion question

1d. Unless you know how to draw out the wisdom and power of God from your spirit, you will end up trying to discern how to follow God's will by what?
   A. What appeals to your mind and emotions most
   B. Advice form a pastor, prophet, or successful business man
   C. Choosing what appears to be the easiest or most practical way
   D. All of the above
   E. None of the above
   D. All of the above

2. Paul said, *"We speak the wisdom of God in a mystery, even the hidden wisdom of God"* (1 Cor. 2:7). Paul says he drew the knowledge out of his spirit by speaking in tongues.

> *For if I pray in an unknown tongue, my spirit prayeth, but my understanding is unfruitful.*
>
> 1 CORINTHIANS 14:14

When we speak in tongues, our spirits pray—the part of us that knows all things (1 John 2:20), is renewed in knowledge (Col. 3:10), and has the mind of Christ (1 Cor. 2:16). Our minds don't understand what we are saying, but Paul tells us how to unravel the mystery:

> *Wherefore let him that speaketh in an unknown tongue pray that he may interpret.*
>
> 1 CORINTHIANS 14:13

All we have to do is ask God to give us an interpretation of what we are praying from our spirits, and He will reveal to us the wisdom we are speaking in tongues. Speaking in tongues isn't just for the purpose of prophecy or ministering to other people.

2a. How did Paul draw knowledge out of his spirit?
   By speaking in tongues

2b. What part of you prays when you pray in tongues?
   A. Your mind
   B. Your spirit
   C. Your stomach
   D. Your soul
   E. Your mouth
   B. Your spirit

2c. What do you have to do to interpret what you're praying from your spirit?
   Ask God to give you an interpretation

2d. True or False: Speaking in tongues isn't just for the purpose of prophecy or ministering to other people.
   True

3.   Every born-again believer who is filled with the Holy Spirit has *the ability* to speak in tongues.

> *And these signs shall follow them that believe; In my name shall they cast out devils; they shall speak with new tongues.*
>
> MARK 16:17

It's not something you do one time in church in order to prove that you are filled with the Holy Spirit; it's something you should be doing on a regular basis. You edify yourself when you speak in tongues (1 Cor. 14:4) and promote spiritual growth. Speaking in tongues is an act of faith; it requires you to cross the barrier between carnal thinking and being focused on God—it is impossible for you to pray in tongues over a long period of time and keep your mind focused on carnal, ungodly things. If you persist in speaking in tongues, your attention will shift to spiritual things—which bring life and peace (Rom. 8:6-7).

3a. Read Mark 16:17. Every _____ who is filled with the Holy Spirit has *the ability* to speak in tongues.
     Believer

3b. True or false: Speaking in tongues is something you do one time in church in order to prove that you are filled with the Holy Spirit.
     False

3c. You should pray in tongues on a _____ basis.
     Regular

3d. Discussion question: What does "edify" and "promote spiritual growth" mean to you?
     Discussion question

3e. Discussion question: What are some experiences that have demonstrated the power of praying in tongues in your life?
     Discussion question

3f. Read Romans 8:6-7. What will happen if you persist in speaking in tongues?
     Your attention will shift to spiritual things—which bring life and peace

4. You can do something with your mind as you pray in tongues and still have perfect comprehension. The mind will wander while you are praying in tongues and start thinking of all sorts of things. What helped me to focus my thoughts on God was to pray with my mind as I prayed with my spirit. As I prayed, things would suddenly come to me. I would think of people I hadn't thought of in years. So, I would pray for them with my mind—at the same time I was praying in tongues out of my mouth. I would call the person and talk to them, and each time, it was an answer to prayer. *When you pray in tongues, God will speak to you and reveal things that you can't know with your physical mind.*

4a. True or false: Your mind will wander while you are praying in tongues if you don't focus your thoughts on God.
True

4b. Discussion question: Why do you think Andrew experienced what he did when he focused his thoughts on God while he prayed in tongues?
Discussion question

DISCIPLESHIP QUESTIONS • 10.1

1. Discussion question: Why is it important to not build a doctrine around one verse but to keep reading?

   _____

   _____

   _____

2. You can _____ the things of God.

3. Discussion question: How would you apply 1 John 2:20 to your life?

   _____

   _____

   _____

4. Unless you know how to draw out the wisdom and power of God from your spirit, you will end up trying to discern how to follow God's will by what?
   A. What appeals to your mind and emotions most
   B. Advice form a pastor, prophet, or successful business man
   C. Choosing what appears to be the easiest or most practical way
   D. All of the above
   E. None of the above

5. How did Paul draw knowledge out of his spirit?

   _____

   _____

   _____

6. What part of you prays when you pray in tongues?

   _____

   _____

   _____

7. What do you have to do to interpret what you're praying from your spirit?

_____

_____

_____

8. True or False: Speaking in tongues isn't just for the purpose of prophecy or ministering to other people.

9. Read Mark 16:17. Every _____ who is filled with the Holy Spirit has *the ability* to speak in tongues.

10. True or false: Speaking in tongues is something you do one time in church in order to prove that you are filled with the Holy Spirit.

11. You should pray in tongues on a _____ basis.

12. Discussion question: What does "edify" and "promote spiritual growth" mean to you?

_____

_____

_____

13. Discussion question: What are some experiences that have demonstrated the power of praying in tongues in your life?

_____

_____

_____

14. Read Romans 8:6-7. What will happen if you persist in speaking in tongues?

_____

_____

_____

15. True or false: Your mind will wander while you are praying in tongues if you don't focus your thoughts on God.

16. Discussion question: Why do you think Andrew experienced what he did when he focused his thoughts on God while he prayed in tongues?

_____

_____

_____

ANSWER KEY • 10.1

1. *Discussion question*
2. Understand
3. *Discussion question*
4. D. All of the above
5. By speaking in tongues
6. B. Your spirit
7. Ask God to give you an interpretation
8. True
9. Believer
10. False
11. Regular
12. *Discussion question*
13. *Discussion question*
14. Your attention will shift to spiritual things—which bring life and peace
15. True
16. *Discussion question*

SCRIPTURES • 10.1

1 CORINTHIANS 2:9-12
But as it is written, Eye hath not seen, nor ear heard, neither have entered into the heart of man, the things which God hath prepared for them that love him. [10] But God hath revealed them unto us by his Spirit: for the Spirit searcheth all things, yea, the deep things of God. [11] For what man knoweth the things of a man, save the spirit of man which is in him? even so the things of God knoweth no man, but the Spirit of God. [12] Now we have received, not the spirit of the world, but the spirit which is of God; that we might know the things that are freely given to us of God.

ISAIAH 55:8-9
For my thoughts are not your thoughts, neither are your ways my ways, saith the Lord. [9] For as the heavens are higher than the earth, so are my ways higher than your ways, and my thoughts than your thoughts.

JAMES 1:5
If any of you lack wisdom, let him ask of God, that giveth to all men liberally, and upbraideth not; and it shall be given him.

EPHESIANS 1:8
Wherein he hath abounded toward us in all wisdom and prudence.

1 JOHN 2:20
But ye have an unction from the Holy One, and ye know all things.

PSALM 32:8-9
I will instruct thee and teach thee in the way which thou shalt go: I will guide thee with mine eye. [9] Be ye not as the horse, or as the mule, which have no understanding: whose mouth must be held in with bit and bridle, lest they come near unto thee.

ISAIAH 30:21
And thine ears shall hear a word behind thee, saying, This is the way, walk ye in it, when ye turn to the right hand, and when ye turn to the left.

1 KINGS 19:12-13
And after the earthquake a fire; but the Lord was not in the fire: and after the fire a still small voice. [13] And it was so, when Elijah heard it, that he wrapped his face in his mantle, and went out, and stood in the entering in of the cave. And, behold, there came a voice unto him, and said, What doest thou here, Elijah?

ACTS 16:9
And a vision appeared to Paul in the night; There stood a man of Macedonia, and prayed him, saying, Come over into Macedonia, and help us.

ACTS 16:22-24
And the multitude rose up together against them: and the magistrates rent off their clothes, and commanded to beat them. [23] And when they had laid many stripes upon them, they cast them into prison, charging the jailor to keep them safely: [24] Who, having received such a charge, thrust them into the inner prison, and made their feet fast in the stocks.

COLOSSIANS 3:10
And have put on the new man, which is renewed in knowledge after the image of him that created him.

1 CORINTHIANS 2:16
For who hath known the mind of the Lord, that he may instruct him? But we have the mind of Christ.

1 CORINTHIANS 2:6-7
Howbeit we speak wisdom among them that are perfect: yet not the wisdom of this world, nor of the princes of this world, that come to nought: [7] But we speak the wisdom of God in a mystery, even the hidden wisdom, which God ordained before the world unto our glory.

PHILIPPIANS 4:19
But my God shall supply all your need according to his riches in glory by Christ Jesus.

1 CORINTHIANS 14:1-2
Follow after charity, and desire spiritual gifts, but rather that ye may prophesy. [2] For he that speaketh in an unknown tongue speaketh not unto men, but unto God: for no man understandeth him; howbeit in the spirit he speaketh mysteries.

ACTS 17:6
And when they found them not, they drew Jason and certain brethren unto the rulers of the city, crying, These that have turned the world upside down are come hither also.

1 CORINTHIANS 14:13-14
Wherefore let him that speaketh in an unknown tongue pray that he may interpret. [14] For if I pray in an unknown tongue, my spirit prayeth, but my understanding is unfruitful.

1 CORINTHIANS 14:27-28

If any man speak in an unknown tongue, let it be by two, or at the most by three, and that by course; and let one interpret. [28] But if there be no interpreter, let him keep silence in the church; and let him speak to himself, and to God.

1 CORINTHIANS 14:18-19

I thank my God, I speak with tongues more than ye all: [19] Yet in the church I had rather speak five words with my understanding, that by my voice I might teach others also, than ten thousand words in an unknown tongue.

1 CORINTHIANS 12:30

Have all the gifts of healing? do all speak with tongues? do all interpret?

MARK 16:17

And these signs shall follow them that believe; In my name shall they cast out devils; they shall speak with new tongues.

1 CORINTHIANS 2:14

But the natural man receiveth not the things of the Spirit of God: for they are foolishness unto him: neither can he know them, because they are spiritually discerned.

1 CORINTHIANS 4:4

He that speaketh in an unknown tongue edifieth himself; but he that prophesieth edifieth the church.

ROMANS 8:6-7

For to be carnally minded is death; but to be spiritually minded is life and peace. [7] Because the carnal mind is enmity against God: for it is not subject to the law of God, neither indeed can be.

LESSON 10.2

Supernatural things happen when you pray in tongues. As you pray, God will speak things to you. Interpretation doesn't mean you pray in tongues one moment and then ask for an interpretation in English right after. As you pray in tongues, your understanding will become fruitful. You will get a mental understanding of the things your spirit is praying; it's the hidden wisdom of God being drawn out into your natural awareness.

For about the first two years that I spoke in tongues, I had doubts that it was really God. I was raised a Baptist and had been told that the devil will give you a "demon tongue." I still had those thoughts come to me after being baptized in the Holy Spirit. Even though I knew speaking in tongues was from God, I wasn't totally confident.

One morning, I prayed in tongues for two hours and fought thoughts of unbelief the whole time. I was thinking, *Is this really God? Is this really the Holy Spirit? Or am I just making this stuff up?* As I was praying, a man I hadn't seen in four years knocked on my door. He was crying. He just walked in, sat down, and started telling me his problems. My first thought was that I had wasted the previous two hours praying in tongues, when I could have been doing something really spiritual that might have helped this guy. But then I realized I wouldn't even have known to pray for him. I hadn't seen or even thought of him in four years. Suddenly, it dawned on me that I had been praying in tongues for him for the previous two hours.

Immediately, I knew his problems. I stopped him in mid-sentence and said, "Let me tell you what's going on." I told him what was wrong, and he was totally shocked. He knew it had to be God because there was no way I could have known what was happening. He knew God was speaking to him. As soon as he understood that God was supernaturally working in his situation, he was totally set free. It was a confirmation to him that I wasn't merely giving him advice but that the Holy Spirit was interpreting the situation. I was able to minister to him from the power of God instead of from my own wisdom and understanding. Those two hours of speaking in tongues had paid off, even when I was struggling with doubt.

This is why getting a mental understanding of the things you are praying about in tongues is important. You don't need to stop and receive a "word-for-word" interpretation as you pray; you only have to be inspired in your thoughts. Whenever I don't know what to do, I pray in tongues and ask God for an interpretation. I say, "Father, give me wisdom. Show me what I need to know." I know wisdom resides in my spirit, and I pray it out by speaking in tongues and receiving an interpretation. It results in supernatural revelation.

Some of you may think, *I wonder if these stories are really proof that speaking in tongues is from God? Maybe those were just coincidences.* If I had the space, I could give you hundreds of examples that prove speaking in tongues is from God. You are too late to try to convince me that this doesn't work. I know it works. It has been working in my life for a long, *long* time.

Earlier I wrote about needing 3.2 million dollars to renovate our building in Colorado Springs, CO. When the banker told me we were going to have to start the loan process all over, I prayed. I was busy at the office, so I didn't hear anything right then. Once I got home, I went for a walk on my property. As I walked, I prayed in tongues and asked for an interpretation. I wasn't even ten minutes down the trail before a prophecy came back to mind that I didn't need a bank—my partners would be my bank. I had thoughts come to me that hadn't crossed my mind in over a year—revelations that ultimately solved my problem. All of the renovation was completed without taking out a loan because I prayed in tongues and God gave me wisdom how to do it.

Power for Living

When you have a need, don't ask God for help and then wait around to hear an audible voice echo down from the heavens. In your spirit, you have the mind of Christ. All you have to do is pray in tongues and ask for interpretation. Your spirit will intercede for you and pray exactly what you need to know. The answer may not come within the first five minutes. It may take a period of time. Like I said, it took me two years to get to where praying in tongues was deeply confirmed in me and I didn't have any more doubts. It may take a period of time for you to get your mind renewed enough in faith that you can truly focus on God while speaking in tongues. Nonetheless, in your spirit, you have the hidden wisdom of God, and praying in tongues will draw it out.

I believe this is how the Apostle Paul received his revelation of God's grace. He wrote in his letter to the Galatians that when he was converted, he didn't go back to Jerusalem. He didn't receive his revelation from the disciples, or any other man; he received it directly from God (Gal. 1:11-12). Paul spent three and a half years praying in the desert to get his revelation (Gal. 1:17-19). I believe he was praying in tongues and drawing that revelation out of his spirit.

The Jews of that time memorized the first five books of the Bible, so Paul already knew the Old Testament scriptures inside and out. He had knowledge of God's Word, but he needed to understand it—so he prayed in tongues. He said the message he preached was the hidden wisdom of God in a mystery (1 Cor. 2:6-7); by praying in tongues, he was praying the hidden wisdom of God out of his spirit. As Paul prayed, God gave him a revelation of grace that is still transforming lives.

The Apostle Peter wrote in his letter that Paul's letters contained *"things hard to be understood."* The unlearned, or carnal people, wrestled with this along with the other scriptures (2 Pet. 3:16). Peter confirmed that Paul's writings were Scripture and said they were hard to understand. Peter was a man who lived with Jesus twenty-four hours a day for more than three years, yet he didn't understand the grace of God at the level Paul did.

One time, Paul actually had to rebuke Peter openly for mistreating the Gentile believers (Gal. 2:11). Paul had a greater revelation of the grace of God and true nature of Jesus than people who lived with Him because he received his revelation by the spirit—not by observation or intellect. It's possible that there was more involved in receiving his revelation than praying in tongues. We don't know, but I believe that speaking in tongues was a large part of it. Without a doubt, we can know things by the spirit better than we can by sight, feeling, or our carnal minds.

We aren't just natural beings; we are supernatural. When we get born again, we become new creatures (2 Cor. 5:17). We have power on the inside of us. We have the Spirit of God living on the inside of us (1 Cor. 6:19). Many Christians feel powerless to make changes in their lives, but that isn't true. We have God's power and authority that Jesus purchased for us when He died on the cross. Once we know who we are and how to release the power of God within us, sickness and poverty don't stand a chance. I believe that praying in tongues is essential in releasing what's in our spirits. It will make our understanding fruitful, and God will give us revelation.

Often when I pray in tongues, I don't get a specific revelation instantly. But later, for instance, when I go to a large meeting and am praying for people, the Lord will show me things and give me words of knowledge—He will show me things about people that I couldn't possibly know by my own natural understanding. Those words of knowledge enable me to call out specific healings the Lord is performing. It also builds people's faith, and miracles begin to happen. I'm not special; I just pray in tongues and God shows me what I need to know when the time comes.

Praying in Tongues Is for Today's Church

I pray in tongues all the time. Many people don't understand how important praying in tongues is. The devil has fought speaking in tongues because he knows how powerful it is. Religious people will sometimes say that speaking in tongues is "of the devil." But if speaking in tongues is of the devil, why can't you go into a bar and hear people speaking in tongues? Why don't criminals pray in tongues? It's an argument that doesn't even make sense. The Bible specifically says, *"Forbid not to speak with tongues"* (1 Cor. 14:39). It is a command from God, but many religious people say speaking in tongues passed away with the apostles.

The Bible says that speaking in tongues will not pass away until that which is perfect has come (1 Cor. 13:10). Some try to argue that speaking in tongues has passed away because *"that which is perfect"* is the Bible. I agree that the Bible is perfect, but that is not what this scripture is talking about. The Scripture says we will see the Lord *"face to face" and* knowledge will pass away at the same time as speaking in tongues passes away (1 Cor 13:8-12). But we haven't seen Jesus face to face, and knowledge hasn't passed away.

"That which is perfect" is our glorified bodies. Therefore, that verse is saying that speaking in tongues will pass away when Jesus comes. We won't need to speak in tongues in heaven, because our carnal nature will be gone, allowing our spirits to dominate. But until that time, we need to continue to pray in tongues.

Speaking in tongues empowers us to discern and follow God's will. *In our spirits, we have everything we need to follow God's will*—we just aren't using it. We love the light of our television more than we love the light of God's Word. When we spend time praying in tongues, getting our minds focused on the Lord and asking Him for wisdom, He will lead and guide us. We need to ask the Lord to reveal what we are praying in tongues and we will see supernatural things start to happen.

Now, let me put one qualification on this: Don't pray in tongues and then assume that the first thought that comes to your mind is from God. It has to match up with the nature and the will of God as expressed through His Word. If your first thought after speaking in tongues is *I think I need a new spouse,* then that's not from God. God's leading will never be contrary to His Word. When you first get started in discerning God's leading, it's a good idea to have mature Christians in your life who can help you judge whether or not the desires you have are from God. As with all spiritual things, there is a maturation process involved in speaking in tongues.

I promise you that praying in tongues merely during the time you spend commuting to work in your car can transform you. You could change your life by spending no more time praying in tongues than you already spend sitting in traffic. Pray in tongues instead of listening to junk on the radio talking about falling off some bar stool, your dog leaving, losing your truck, or everything else. You are sitting in traffic anyway, so you don't have much else to do. Use that time to build yourself up and promote spiritual growth.

OUTLINE • 10.2

V. Supernatural things happen when you pray in tongues—God will speak things to you.

   A. Interpretation doesn't mean you pray in tongues one moment and then ask for an interpretation in English right after.

   B. You will get a mental understanding of the things your spirit is praying; it's the hidden wisdom of God being drawn out into your natural awareness.

   C. Even though I knew speaking in tongues was from God, I wasn't totally confident, until I the morning I was able to minister to my friend from the power of God instead of from my own wisdom and understanding.

   D. I know wisdom resides in my spirit, and I pray it out by speaking in tongues and receiving an interpretation—it results in supernatural revelation.

VI. When Paul was converted, he didn't receive his revelation from the disciples, or any other man; he received it directly from God (Gal. 1:11-12).

   A. He spent three and a half years praying in the desert to get his revelation (Gal. 1:17-19).

   B. I believe he was praying in tongues and drawing that revelation out of his spirit.

   C. As Paul prayed, God gave him a revelation of grace that is still transforming lives.

   D. Paul had a greater revelation of the grace of God and true nature of Jesus than people who lived with Him because he received his revelation by the spirit—not by observation or intellect.

VII. We aren't just natural beings; we are supernatural.

   A. Many Christians feel powerless to make changes in their lives, but that isn't true— we have God's power and authority that Jesus purchased for us when He died on the cross.

   B. Once we know who we are and how to release the power of God within us, sickness and poverty don't stand a chance.

   C. I believe that praying in tongues is essential in releasing what's in our spirits.

VIII. Many people don't understand how important praying in tongues is.

   A. The devil has fought speaking in tongues because he knows how powerful it is.

   B. The Bible specifically says, *"Forbid not to speak with tongues"* (1 Cor. 14:39).

   C. First Corinthians 13:10 says that speaking in tongues will not pass away until that which is perfect has come.

D. *"That which is perfect"* is our glorified bodies; therefore, that verse is saying that speaking in tongues will pass away when Jesus comes.

E. When we have our glorified, bodies we will no longer need to speak in tongues because our carnal nature will be gone.

F. Speaking in tongues empowers us to discern and follow God's will.

G. When we spend time praying in tongues, getting our minds focused on the Lord and asking Him for wisdom, He will lead and guide us.

IX. Now, let me put one qualification on this: Don't pray in tongues and then assume that the first thought that comes to your mind is from God.

A. It has to match up with the nature and the will of God as expressed through His Word.

B. When you first get started in discerning God's leading, it's a good idea to have mature Christians in your life who can help you judge whether or not the desires you have are from God.

C. As with all spiritual things, there is a maturation process involved in speaking in tongues.

X. I promise you that praying in tongues merely during the time you spend commuting to work in your car can transform you.

A. Pray in tongues instead of listening to junk on the radio talking about falling off of some bar stool, your dog leaving, losing your truck, or everything else.

B. Use that time to build yourself up and promote spiritual growth.

5. Supernatural things happen when you pray in tongues—God will speak things to you. Interpretation doesn't mean you pray in tongues one moment and then ask for an interpretation in English right after. You will get a mental understanding of the things your spirit is praying; it's the hidden wisdom of God being drawn out into your natural awareness. Even though I knew speaking in tongues was from God, I wasn't totally confident, until I the morning I was able to minister to my friend from the power of God instead of from my own wisdom and understanding. I know wisdom resides in my spirit, and I pray it out by speaking in tongues and receiving an interpretation—it results in supernatural revelation.

5a. True or false: God will speak things to you when you pray in tongues.
   True

5b. What will you get when you ask for an interpretation?
   A mental understanding of the things your spirit is praying

5c. Another way to call this is what?
   A. Going with the first thought that springs to mind
   B. Just guessing
   C. A supernatural revelation
   D. All of the above
   E. None of the above
   C. A supernatural revelation

6. When Paul was converted, he didn't receive his revelation from the disciples, or any other man; he received it directly from God (Gal. 1:11-12). He spent three and a half years praying in the desert to get his revelation (Gal. 1:17-19). I believe he was praying in tongues and drawing that revelation out of his spirit. As Paul prayed, God gave him a revelation of grace that is still transforming lives. Paul had a greater revelation of the grace of God and true nature of Jesus than people who lived with Him because he received his revelation by the spirit—not by observation or intellect.

6a. Andrew believes Paul was praying in tongues and drawing revelation out of his spirit that is _____ transforming lives.
   Still

6b. Discussion question: What are some examples where God gave you revelation and it wasn't by observation or intellect?
   Discussion question

7. We aren't just natural beings; we are supernatural. Many Christians feel powerless to make changes in their lives, but that isn't true—we have God's power and authority that Jesus purchased for us when He died on the cross. Once we know who we are and how to release the power of God within us, sickness and poverty don't stand a chance. I believe that praying in tongues is essential in releasing what's in our spirits.

7a. If you have God's power and authority that Jesus purchased for you when He died on the cross, what can you do?
Make changes in your life

7b. Discussion question: "Once we know who we are and how to release the power of God within us, sickness and poverty don't stand a chance." How has this been true in your life?
Discussion question

7c. What's essential in releasing what's in your spirit?
    A. The perfect opportunity
    B. Exercising
    C. What you eat
    D. Going to church
    E. Praying in tongues
    E. Praying in tongues

8. Many people don't understand how important praying in tongues is. The devil has fought speaking in tongues because he knows how powerful it is. The Bible specifically says, *"Forbid not to speak with tongues"* (1 Cor. 14:39). First Corinthians 13:10 says that speaking in tongues will not pass away until that which is perfect has come. *"That which is perfect"* is our glorified bodies; therefore, that verse is saying that speaking in tongues will pass away when Jesus comes. When we have our glorified, bodies we will no longer need to speak in tongues because our carnal nature will be gone. Speaking in tongues empowers us to discern and follow God's will. When we spend time praying in tongues, getting our minds focused on the Lord and asking Him for wisdom, He will lead and guide us.

8a. According to 1 Corinthians 14:39, what shouldn't you do?
Forbid speaking in tongues

8b. True or False: Tongues must have passed away, since not everyone agrees concerning it.
False

8c. Read 1 Corinthians 13:10. True or false: *"That which is perfect"* is your glorified body; therefore, that verse is saying that speaking in tongues passed away with the apostles.
False

8d. Speaking in tongues empowers you to what?
    A. Discern and follow God's will
    B. Discern and follow church culture
    C. Discern and follow a vision
    D. All of the above
    E. None of the above
    A. Discern and follow God's will

9. Now, let me put one qualification on this: Don't pray in tongues and then assume that the first thought that comes to your mind is from God. It has to match up with the nature and the will of God as expressed through His Word. When you first get started in discerning God's leading, it's a good idea to have mature Christians in your life who can help you judge whether or not the desires you have are from God. As with all spiritual things, there is a maturation process involved in speaking in tongues.

9a.   Why shouldn't you assume that the first thought that comes to your mind is from God?
Because has to match up with the nature and the will of God as expressed through His Word

9b.   Discussion question: Why do thoughts that come to your mind have to match up with the nature and the will of God as expressed through His Word?
Discussion question

9c.   What is a good idea when you first get started in discerning God's leading?
To have mature Christians in your life who can help you judge whether or not the desires you have are from God

10. I promise you that praying in tongues merely during the time you spend commuting to work in your car can transform you. Pray in tongues instead of listening to junk on the radio talking about falling off of some bar stool, your dog leaving, losing your truck, or everything else. Use that time to build yourself up and promote spiritual growth.

10a.   Praying in tongues merely during the time you spend commuting to work in your car can _____ you.
Transform

10b.   Discussion question: What are some examples from your life where praying in tongues, even if it was for a short time, has made a difference in your life?
Discussion question

17. True or false: God will speak things to you when you pray in tongues.

18. What will you get when you ask for an interpretation?

_____

_____

_____

19. Another way to call this is what?
    A. Going with the first thought that springs to mind
    B. Just guessing
    C. A supernatural revelation
    D. All of the above
    E. None of the above

20. Andrew believes Paul was praying in tongues and drawing revelation out of his spirit that is _____ transforming lives.

21. Discussion question: What are some examples where God gave you revelation and it wasn't by observation or intellect?

_____

_____

_____

22. If you have God's power and authority that Jesus purchased for you when He died on the cross, what can you do?

_____

_____

_____

23. Discussion question: "Once we know who we are and how to release the power of God within us, sickness and poverty don't stand a chance." How has this been true in your life?

_____

_____

_____

24. What's essential in releasing what's in your spirit?
    A. The perfect opportunity
    B. Exercising
    C. What you eat
    D. Going to church
    E. Praying in tongues

25. According to 1 Corinthians 14:39, what shouldn't you do?

    _____

    _____

    _____

26. True or False: Tongues must have passed away, since not everyone agrees concerning it.

27. Read 1 Corinthians 13:10. True or false: *"That which is perfect"* is your glorified body; therefore, that verse is saying that speaking in tongues passed away with the apostles.

    _____

    _____

    _____

28. Speaking in tongues empowers you to what?
    A. Discern and follow God's will
    B. Discern and follow church culture
    C. Discern and follow a vision
    D. All of the above
    E. None of the above

29. Why shouldn't you assume that the first thought that comes to your mind is from God?

    _____

    _____

    _____

30. Discussion question: Why do thoughts that come to your mind have to match up with the nature and the will of God as expressed through His Word?

_____

_____

_____

31. What is a good idea when you first get started in discerning God's leading?

_____

_____

_____

32. Praying in tongues merely during the time you spend commuting to work in your car can _____ you.

33. Discussion question: What are some examples from your life where praying in tongues, even if it was for a short time, has made a difference in your life?

_____

_____

_____

17. True
18. A mental understanding of the things your spirit is praying
19. C. A supernatural revelation
20. Still
21. *Discussion question*
22. Make changes in your life
23. *Discussion question*
24. E. Praying in tongues
25. Forbid speaking in tongues
26. False
27. False
28. A. Discern and follow God's will
29. Because has to match up with the nature and the will of God as expressed through His Word
30. *Discussion question*
31. To have mature Christians in your life who can help you judge whether or not the desires you have are from God
32. Transform
33. *Discussion question*

GALATIANS 1:11-12
But I certify you, brethren, that the gospel which was preached of me is not after man. [12] For I neither received it of man, neither was I taught it, but by the revelation of Jesus Christ.

GALATIANS 1:17-19
Neither went I up to Jerusalem to them which were apostles before me; but I went into Arabia, and returned again unto Damascus. [18] Then after three years I went up to Jerusalem to see Peter, and abode with him fifteen days. [19] But other of the apostles saw I none, save James the Lord's brother.

1 CORINTHIANS 2:6-7
Howbeit we speak wisdom among them that are perfect: yet not the wisdom of this world, nor of the princes of this world, that come to nought: [7] But we speak the wisdom of God in a mystery, even the hidden wisdom, which God ordained before the world unto our glory.

2 PETER 3:16
As also in all his epistles, speaking in them of these things; in which are some things hard to be understood, which they that are unlearned and unstable wrest, as they do also the other scriptures, unto their own destruction.

2 CORINTHIANS 5:17
Therefore if any man be in Christ, he is a new creature: old things are passed away; behold, all things are become new.

1 CORINTHIANS 6:19
What? know ye not that your body is the temple of the Holy Ghost which is in you, which ye have of God, and ye are not your own?

1 CORINTHIANS 14:39
Wherefore, brethren, covet to prophesy, and forbid not to speak with tongues.

1 CORINTHIANS 13:10
But when that which is perfect is come, then that which is in part shall be done away.

LESSON 10.3

The Baptism of the Holy Spirit

But ye shall receive power, after that the Holy Ghost is come upon you: and ye shall be witnesses unto me both in Jerusalem, and in all Judaea, and in Samaria, and unto the uttermost part of the earth.

ACTS 1:8

If you don't have this gift of speaking in tongues, you need it. God has placed Himself on the inside of every born-again believer, but there's more to the Christian life than the initial born-again experience. You need the baptism of the Holy Spirit to draw out the power God has placed inside of you and to pray in tongues. Speaking in tongues isn't something you do just to have a shiver run up and down your spine or to feel the presence of the Lord; it's much more powerful than that. You need the baptism of the Holy Spirit in order to be an effective witness and flow in the gifts of the Spirit.

Jesus told His disciples, *"Behold, I send the promise of my Father upon you: but tarry ye in the city of Jerusalem, until ye be endued with power from on high"* (Luke 24:49). Jesus didn't want the disciples out on their own trying to advance His kingdom; He wanted them to be filled with the power of the Holy Spirit. In every example in the book of Acts where people received the Holy Spirit, it is either stated or implied in the text that they spoke in tongues. Speaking in tongues *is* the initial outward sign of the baptism of the Holy Spirit.

You don't need to *"tarry"* until the Lord deems you worthy to be filled with the Holy Spirit. Some churches teach that you have to get every sin out of your life before God will baptize you in the Holy Spirit. They teach that you can't have any problems, because God won't fill a dirty vessel. But God doesn't have any other kind of vessel to fill! If you could get holy without the Holy Spirit—you wouldn't *need* the Holy Spirit. The very fact that you have problems means that you are a candidate to receive the Holy Spirit. Don't let some failure make you think God won't fill you with His Spirit.

> *What? know ye not that your body is the temple of the Holy Ghost which is in you, which ye have of God, and ye are not your own?*
>
> 1 CORINTHIANS 6:19

The Word of God says that you become the temple of the living God when you are born again. God made you so He could fill you with His power. So, there is no way He would refuse to give you the Holy Spirit. You were *created* to be God's temple. He wants to fill you with the Holy Spirit more than you want to be filled.

> *If a son shall ask bread of any of you that is a father, will he give him a stone? or if he ask a fish, will he for a fish give him a serpent? [12] Or if he shall ask an egg, will he offer him a scorpion? [13] If ye then, being evil, know how to give good gifts unto your children: how much more shall your heavenly Father give the Holy Spirit to them that ask him?*
>
> LUKE 11:11-13

You don't need to beg and plead for God to baptize you with the Holy Spirit—you just have to be born again. Jesus is the one who baptizes you in the Holy Spirit, but the world cannot receive Him (John 14:16-17). No Jesus—no Holy Spirit. But if you are born again, God wants you to be filled with the power of the Holy Spirit with the evidence of speaking in tongues. God wants it and you need it. You might be thinking, *Do I have to speak in tongues?* No, you don't have to—you *get* to. It isn't a requirement for being saved; it's a benefit.

I guarantee that you are going to need the baptism of the Holy Spirit to find, follow, and fulfill God's will for your life. You can't do it on your own. The Holy Spirit will guide you and show you things coming down the pike (John 16:13). The Holy Spirit is sent to reveal Jesus. He is your Teacher (John 14:26). You need His power in your life to accomplish God's plans for you.

One thing you need to understand about speaking in tongues is that the Holy Spirit inspires the words, but *you* have to speak them. The Holy Spirit isn't going to take control of your body and speak for you. God is a gentleman. He doesn't force Himself on anyone—He doesn't take control of people.

> *And they were all filled with the Holy Ghost, and began to speak with other tongues, as the Spirit gave them utterance.*
>
> ACTS 2:4

The Spirit gave utterance, but the believers did the speaking. The Holy Spirit inspires you to speak, but you have to open up your mouth and utter the sounds. It is going to be your voice, affected by your accent. It's an act of faith: The Holy Spirit inspires—by faith, you do the speaking.

For example, when I minister, I believe God is speaking through me. But He doesn't take my mouth and make me speak. If I prayed and asked God to speak through me and to not let me say anything wrong—and then just opened my mouth and waited on Him to make it move—nothing would happen. It doesn't happen that way. When I speak, words come out in my Texan accent with my sense of humor and personality. But I believe it's inspired of God.

Likewise, when you speak in tongues, God doesn't force you to do it. You can't talk in tongues with your mouth closed; you have to open your mouth, begin to make sounds, and believe, by faith, that God is inspiring it. Don't worry about what it sounds like. I've heard that some tribes only speak in clicks of the tongue and others in just different whistles. But they are known languages.

Sometimes speaking in tongues starts out in the same way as when little children learn to talk. Their words may not sound like "Mommy" or "Daddy," but their parents know what they are trying to say. In the same way, our heavenly Father listens to our hearts and loves that we are trying to communicate with Him from our spirits. As we keep praying in tongues, our prayer languages will become more fluent over time—just like a child's does. We just start speaking and don't quit.

God gives the Holy Spirit to everyone who asks of Him. If you recognize that you need the Holy Spirit and want to be filled with His presence, then say the prayer at the end of this chapter. It's the same prayer I have used to see thousands of people receive the baptism of the Holy Spirit.

Don't judge whether or not you receive the Holy Spirit by how you feel when you pray. Some people have great emotional experiences when they are filled with the Holy Spirit, while others don't. I didn't feel a thing—but I received the Holy Spirit. He lives on the inside of me. *God is going to give you the Holy Spirit when you ask,* so you only need to ask once—you don't need to beg. Trust that God has given you the Holy Spirit, whether you feel anything or not. Say this prayer one time, and then begin to thank Him for filling you with the Holy Spirit.

Father, I thank you that I am the temple of the Holy Spirit. I now open up the doors of this temple. Holy Spirit, I welcome You to come fill me and give me supernatural power. I welcome You to renew my mind so that I can think supernaturally instead of naturally and see Your power released into my life. And I ask for this gift of speaking in tongues. I pray this in Jesus' name. Amen.

Rejoice!

If you prayed that prayer and believed in your heart, you are now baptized in the Holy Spirit and you have the ability to speak in tongues! Open up your mouth and begin to utter the words that the Holy Spirit is inspiring you to speak. Don't let the fear of sounding silly stop you. The Apostle Paul said that the natural man doesn't understand the things of the spirit because they are foolishness to him (1 Cor. 2:14). Your mind isn't going to understand the words that come from your lips, but that's okay. Speak out the words that you can feel rising up within you, and don't try to interpret them with your natural mind. As you pray, focus your mind on the love God has for you and who the Word of God says you are.

Continue to pray in tongues by faith, and ask God to give you the interpretation. This is going to start you down a road to seeing the supernatural power of God manifest in your life while giving you the ability to follow God's leading with more than just your natural mind.

XI. If you don't have this gift of speaking in tongues, you need it.

    A. God has place Himself on the inside of every believer, but there's more to the Christian life than the initial born-again experience.

    B. You need the baptism of the Holy Spirit in order to be an effective witness and flow in the gifts of the Spirit.

    C. Jesus didn't want the disciples out on their own trying to advance His kingdom (Luke 24:49).

    D. In every example in the book of Acts where the people received the Holy Spirit, it is either stated or implied that they spoke in tongues.

    E. Speaking in tongues *is* the initial outward sign of the baptism of the Holy Spirit.

XII. You don't need to *"tarry"* in order to be filled with the Spirit.

    A. Some churches teach that you have to get every sin out of your life before God will baptize you in the Holy Spirit, that God won't fill a dirty vessel, but God doesn't have any other kind of vessel to fill.

    B. If you could get holy without the Holy Spirit—you wouldn't *need* the Holy Spirit.

    C. Don't let some failure make you think God won't fill you with His Spirit.

XIII. God made you so He could fill you with His power (1 Cor. 6:19), so there is no way He would refuse to give you the Holy Spirit.

    A. He wants to fill you with the Holy Spirit more than you want to be filled.

    If a son shall ask bread of any of you that is a father, will he give him a stone? or if he ask a fish, will he for a fish give him a serpent? [12] Or if he shall ask an egg, will he offer him a scorpion? [13] If ye then, being evil, know how to give good gifts unto your children: how much more shall your heavenly Father give the Holy Spirit to them that ask him?

                                                        LUKE 11:11-13

    B. You don't need to beg and plead for God to baptize you with the Holy Spirit—you just have to be born again.

    C. If you are born again, God wants you to be filled with the power of the Holy Spirit with the evidence of speaking in tongues, and you need it.

    D. You don't have to speak in tongues—you *get* to.

XIV. I guarantee that you are going to need the baptism of the Holy Spirit to find, follow, and fulfill God's will for your life.

A. The Holy Spirit will guide you and show you things coming down the pike (John 16:13).

B. He is your Teacher (John 14:26).

C. You need His power in your life to accomplish God's plans for you.

XV. One thing you need to understand about speaking in tongues is that the Holy Spirit inspires the words, but *you* have to speak them (Acts 2:4).

A. The Holy Spirit isn't going to take control of your body and speak for you.

B. It's an act of faith.

C. If I prayed and asked God to speak through me and to not let me say anything wrong—and then just opened my mouth and waited on Him to make it move— nothing would happen.

D. Don't worry about what it sounds like.

E. Just like a parent who knows what their child is trying to say, your heavenly Father listens to your heart and loves that you are trying to communicate with Him from your spirit.

F. *God is going to give you the Holy Spirit when you ask*, so you only need to ask once.

G. Trust that He has given you the Holy Spirit, whether you feel anything or not.

H. Say this prayer one time and then begin to thank Him for filling you with the Holy Spirit:

Father, I thank you that I am the temple of the Holy Spirit. I now open up the doors of this temple. Holy Spirit, I welcome You to come fill me and give me supernatural power. I welcome You to renew my mind so that I can think supernaturally instead of naturally and see Your power released into my life. And I ask for this gift of speaking in tongues. I pray this in Jesus' name. Amen.

11. If you don't have this gift of speaking in tongues, you need it. God has place Himself on the inside of every believer, but there's more to the Christian life than the initial born-again experience. You need the baptism of the Holy Spirit in order to be an effective witness and flow in the gifts of the Spirit. Jesus didn't want the disciples out on their own trying to advance His kingdom (Luke 24:49). In every example in the book of Acts where the people received the Holy Spirit, it is either stated or implied that they spoke in tongues. Speaking in tongues *is* the initial outward sign of the baptism of the Holy Spirit.

11a. If you don't have this gift of speaking in tongues, you _____ it.
Need

11b. True or false: It would have been fine if the disciples had gone out on their own trying to advance Jesus' kingdom.
False

11c. In the book of Acts, people recognized the infilling of the Spirit because of what?
   A. They stopped to take communion
   B. Halos floated over the peoples' heads
   C. They were slain in the spirit
   D. They spoke in tongues
   E. They knew the holy hand shake
   D. They spoke in tongues

12. You don't need to *"tarry"* in order to be filled with the Spirit. Some churches teach that you have to get every sin out of your life before God will baptize you in the Holy Spirit, that God won't fill a dirty vessel, but God doesn't have any other kind of vessel to fill. If you could get holy without the Holy Spirit—you wouldn't *need* the Holy Spirit. Don't let some failure make you think God won't fill you with His Spirit.

12a. Discussion question: Why don't you need to *"tarry"* to be filled with the Spirit?
Discussion question

12b. True or False: You have to get every sin out of your life before God will baptize you in the Holy Spirit.
False

12c. Don't let some failure make you _____ God won't fill you with His Spirit.
Think

13. God made you so He could fill you with His power (1 Cor. 6:19), so there is no way He would refuse to give you the Holy Spirit. He wants to fill you with the Holy Spirit more than you want to be filled.

> *If a son shall ask bread of any of you that is a father, will he give him a stone? or if he ask a fish, will he for a fish give him a serpent? [12] Or if he shall ask an egg, will he offer him a scorpion? [13] If ye then, being evil, know how to give good gifts unto your children: how much more shall your heavenly Father give the Holy Spirit to them that ask him?*
>
> LUKE 11:11-13

You don't need to beg and plead for God to baptize you with the Holy Spirit—you just have to be born again. If you are born again, God wants you to be filled with the power of the Holy Spirit with the evidence of speaking in tongues, and you need it. You don't have to speak in tongues—you *get* to.

13a. Read 1 Corinthians 6:19. God _____ you so He could fill you with His power.
Made

13b. In order for God to baptize you with the Holy Spirit, you just have to be what?
A. Hungry
B. Educated
C. Born again
D. All of the above
E. None of the above
C. Born again

13c. God wants you to be filled with _____ _____ _____ _____ _____ _____, and you _____ it.
The power of the Holy Spirit / need

13d. You don't have to speak in tongues—you _____ to.
Get

14. I guarantee that you are going to need the baptism of the Holy Spirit to find, follow, and fulfill God's will for your life. The Holy Spirit will guide you and show you things coming down the pike (John 16:13). He is your Teacher (John 14:26). You need His power in your life to accomplish God's plans for you.

14a. Discussion question: Why do you think the Holy Spirit is essential find, follow, and fulfill God's will?
Discussion question

15. One thing you need to understand about speaking in tongues is that the Holy Spirit inspires the words, but *you* have to speak them (Acts 2:4). The Holy Spirit isn't going to take control of your body and speak for you. It's an act of faith. If I prayed and asked God to speak through me and to not let me say anything wrong—and then just opened my mouth and waited on Him to make it move—nothing would happen. Don't worry about what it sounds like. Just like a parent who knows what their child is trying to say, your heavenly Father listens to your heart and loves that you are trying to communicate with Him from your spirit. *God is going to give you the Holy Spirit when you ask*, so you only need to ask once. Trust that He has given you the Holy Spirit, whether you feel anything or not. Say this prayer one time and then begin to thank Him for filling you with the Holy Spirit:

Father, I thank you that I am the temple of the Holy Spirit. I now open up the doors of this temple. Holy Spirit, I welcome You to come fill me and give me supernatural power. I welcome You to renew my mind so that I can think supernaturally instead of naturally and see Your power released into my life. And I ask for this gift of speaking in tongues. I pray this in Jesus' name. Amen.

15a. True or false: The Holy Spirit inspires words, but it's best to hear them in your head and then whisper them to yourself.
False

15b. Read Acts 2:4. Who began to speak with other tongues?
   A. The Holy Spirit
   B. The mute man
   C. Everyone in Jerusalem
   D. All of the above
   E. None of the above
   E. None of the above

15c. Discussion question: Why is it more important that God knows what you are trying to say rather than you "getting all the words right" in tongues?
Discussion question

15d. God is going to give you the Holy Spirit when you _____.
Ask

15e. Why do you need to trust that God has given you the Holy Spirit when you ask?
Because you may or may not feel that you did

34. If you don't have this gift of speaking in tongues, you _____ it.

35. True or false: It would have been fine if the disciples had gone out on their own trying to advance Jesus' kingdom.

36. In the book of Acts, people recognized the infilling of the Spirit because of what?
    A. They stopped to take communion
    B. Halos floated over the peoples' heads
    C. They were slain in the spirit
    D. They spoke in tongues
    E. They knew the holy hand shake

37. Discussion question: Why don't you need to *"tarry"* to be filled with the Spirit?

    _____

    _____

    _____

38. True or False: You have to get every sin out of your life before God will baptize you in the Holy Spirit.

39. Don't let some failure make you _____ God won't fill you with His Spirit.

40. Read 1 Corinthians 6:19. God _____ you so He could fill you with His power.

41. In order for God to baptize you with the Holy Spirit, you just have to be what?
    A. Hungry
    B. Educated
    C. Born again
    D. All of the above
    E. None of the above

42. God wants you to be filled with _____,
    and you _____ it.

43. You don't have to speak in tongues—you _____ to.

44. Discussion question: Why do you think the Holy Spirit is essential find, follow, and fulfill God's will?

_____

_____

_____

45. True or false: The Holy Spirit inspires words, but it's best to hear them in your head and then whisper them to yourself.

46. Read Acts 2:4. Who began to speak with other tongues?
    A. The Holy Spirit
    B. The mute man
    C. Everyone in Jerusalem
    D. All of the above
    E. None of the above

47. Discussion question: Why is it more important that God knows what you are trying to say rather than you "getting all the words right" in tongues?

_____

_____

_____

48. God is going to give you the Holy Spirit when you _____.

49. Why do you need to trust that God has given you the Holy Spirit when you ask?

_____

_____

_____

34. Need
35. False
36. D. They spoke in tongues
37. *Discussion question*
38. False
39. Think
40. Made
41. C. Born again
42. The power of the Holy Spirit / need
43. Get
44. *Discussion question*
45. False
46. E. None of the above
47. *Discussion question*
48. Ask
49. Because you may or may not feel that you did

ACTS 1:8
But ye shall receive power, after that the Holy Ghost is come upon you: and ye shall be witnesses unto me both in Jerusalem, and in all Judaea, and in Samaria, and unto the uttermost part of the earth.

LUKE 24:49
And, behold, I send the promise of my Father upon you: but tarry ye in the city of Jerusalem, until ye be endued with power from on high.

1 CORINTHIANS 6:19
What? know ye not that your body is the temple of the Holy Ghost which is in you, which ye have of God, and ye are not your own?

LUKE 11:11-13
If a son shall ask bread of any of you that is a father, will he give him a stone? or if he ask a fish, will he for a fish give him a serpent? [12] Or if he shall ask an egg, will he offer him a scorpion? [13] If ye then, being evil, know how to give good gifts unto your children: how much more shall your heavenly Father give the Holy Spirit to them that ask him?

JOHN 14:16-17
And I will pray the Father, and he shall give you another Comforter, that he may abide with you for ever; [17] Even the Spirit of truth; whom the world cannot receive, because it seeth him not, neither knoweth him: but ye know him; for he dwelleth with you, and shall be in you.

JOHN 16:13
Howbeit when he, the Spirit of truth, is come, he will guide you into all truth: for he shall not speak of himself; but whatsoever he shall hear, that shall he speak: and he will shew you things to come.

JOHN 14:26
But the Comforter, which is the Holy Ghost, whom the Father will send in my name, he shall teach you all things, and bring all things to your remembrance, whatsoever I have said unto you.

ACTS 2:4
And they were all filled with the Holy Ghost, and began to speak with other tongues, as the Spirit gave them utterance.

1 CORINTHIANS 2:14
But the natural man receiveth not the things of the Spirit of God: for they are foolishness unto him: neither can he know them, because they are spiritually discerned.

RECOMMENDED TEACHINGS

Christian Survival Kit
Jesus knew His disciples would face the most trying time of their lives when He went to the cross. So, He gave them vital survival instructions that apply to your life today!

Item Code: 1001-C   16-CD album

Discover the Keys to Staying Full of God
Staying full of God is not a secret or a mystery; it's simple. For that reason, few people recognize the keys, and even fewer practice them. Learn what they are, and put them into practice. They will keep your heart sensitive.

Item Code: 1029-C   4-CD album
Item Code: 1029-D   As-Seen-on-TV DVD album
Item Code: 324   Paperback
Item Code: 424   Study Guide

Don't Limit God X 10
You are the one who determines who God is and what He can do in your life. He is waiting on you. If you doubt that now, you won't after listening to this message.

Item Code: 1076-C   5-CD album
Item Code: 1076-D   As-Seen-on-TV DVD album
Item Code: 3219-D   Recorded Live DVD album

Effortless Change
We all have areas in our lives we want to change. Trying to change from the outside in is difficult. Inside out is effortless. Learn why.

Item Code: 1018-C   4-CD album
Item Code: 1018-D   As-Seen-on-TV DVD album
Item Code: 331   Paperback
Item Code: 431   Study Guide

God's Man, Plan, and Timing
Moses was God's man, and he knew God's plan, but he didn't have a clue as to the timing or how to see the plan come to pass. This message from Andrew will reveal truths from the Moses' life that will ensure you don't make the same mistakes!

Item Code: U05-C   Single CD

RECOMMENDED TEACHINGS

Hardness of Heart
You might be surprised to find out that all Christians have a degree of hardness in their hearts. Listen as Andrew establishes from Scripture the cause and the cure.

Item Code: 1003-C   4-CD album
Item Code: 1003-D   As-Seen-on-TV DVD album
Item Code: 303   Paperback

Lessons from Elijah
You don't have to experience everything to learn life's lessons. Elijah, a man mightily used of God, is a great example. You'll be blessed from these life examples.

Item Code: 1026-C   5-CD album
Item Code: 1026-D   As-Seen-on-TV DVD album

The Power of Hope
Imagination dictates how your life goes, and if you're ever going to receive what God has for you, you'll need to understand that hope is a *positive* imagination. Learn this and you'll know the true power of hope!

Item Code: 1080-C   5-CD album
Item Code: 1080-D   As-Seen-on-TV DVD album
Item Code: 3221-D   Recorded Live DVD album